getting a **TOP JOB** in
...**MARKETING**

Life is what happens while you are making other plans.

John Lennon

THE TIMES

getting a TOP JOB in ...MARKETING

patrick forsyth

KOGAN
PAGE

First published in 2001

Apart from any fair dealing for the purposes of research or private study, or criticism or review, as permitted under the Copyright, Designs and Patents Act 1988,
this publication may only be reproduced, stored or transmitted, in any form or by
any means, with the prior permission in writing of the publishers, or in the case of
reprographic reproduction in accordance with the terms and licences issued by the
CLA. Enquiries concerning reproduction outside these terms should be sent to the
publishers at the undermentioned address:

Kogan Page Limited
120 Pentonville Road
London N1 9JN

© Patrick Forsyth, 2001

The right of Patrick Forsyth to be identified as the author of this work has been
asserted by him in accordance with the Copyright, Designs and Patents Act 1988.

The views expressed in this book are those of the author, and are not necessarily
the same as those of Times Newspapers Ltd.

British Library Cataloguing in Publication Data

A CIP record for this book is available from the British Library.

ISBN 0 7494 3557 7

Typeset by Saxon Graphics Ltd, Derby
Printed and bound in Great Britain by Clays Ltd, St Ives plc

Contents

The author

Patrick Forsyth has himself had a successful career in marketing; or certainly he likes to think so. He now runs his own company, Touchstone Training & Consultancy, specialising in the improvement of marketing, sales and communications skills, and says he has now 'found an employer I can really get on with'.

He began his career in publishing (well, books seemed an interesting product), and worked happily in sales, promotion and marketing there before escaping to something better paid just ahead of terminal poverty. He then worked for the Institute of Marketing (now the Chartered Institute), first in research, latterly in the promotion of their training products and publications. He helped set up an export assistance scheme and then moved into consultancy, first in a line management marketing position. Much against his better judgement initially, he was soon persuaded to get involved in client work and began to undertake consulting assignments and conduct training courses.

His work also began to take on an international dimension. He helped set up offices in Brussels and Singapore and began to work and lecture overseas. He still travels regularly, especially to Southeast Asia, and has, over the years, worked in most countries in Continental Europe, including the old Eastern bloc. Other, more occasional, visits have included the United States, Australia, East Africa, Argentina and Borneo.

After some years at director level in a medium-sized marketing consultancy, he set up his own organisation in 1990. He conducts training for organisations in a wide range of industries, and has conducted public courses for such bodies as the Institute of Management, the City University Business School and the London Chamber of Commerce.

In addition, he writes on matters of management and marketing in a variety of business journals and is the author of more than 30 business books (with titles published in more than a dozen languages). Titles that relate to the content of this book include: *Everything You Need to Know about Marketing* (Kogan Page) – a light-hearted review demystifying marketing for the layperson; *Career Skills* (Cassell) – a guide to long-term success; *Understanding Office Politics in a Week* (Hodder & Stoughton); and *30 Minutes before your Job Appraisal* (Kogan Page). He has also written material to accompany a variety of training packages (audio, video etc) and has appeared on television discussing marketing and management (fame at last? – with one broadcast in association with the Executive Business Channel/BBC Open University at 3 am!).

His early career plans included 'avoiding public speaking and writing' (so nothing goes perfectly). Future plans include 'less work and more money' (so the trend is likely to continue). Nothing like this book was around when he went into marketing, or who knows what he might have done? Whatever else, he says he is able to look back at a career that has been 'almost wholly very enjoyable', and which continues to be so.

Acknowledgements

Writing a book such as this has only been possible because of the experience I have had working in the marketing world myself. So thanks are due to many people I have met along the way, and in some cases with whom I remain in contact; our crossing paths has provided – wittingly or otherwise – material and examples that I have drawn on and which are reflected in these pages.

Specific thanks are due to a number of people at the Chartered Institute of Marketing. As a member of many years I suppose I expected certain assistance to be available, but what was provided went well beyond expectation and proved most useful. I spent time in their library, and discussed many aspects of marketing careers and education with members of their executive staff. Thanks are due therefore to their Corporate Marketing Manager, David Wright, and other members of his team including Ian Freeman.

I am especially grateful for their permission to quote from several of their brochures and publications; these are mentioned individually within the text and include in some cases a recommendation that readers consider acquiring the publication.

Finally, a word of thanks to publishers Kogan Page. I have written on various aspects of marketing in the past, but the idea for this text was very much their initiative. I am grateful to Philip Mudd for introducing the idea to me and for his support along the way as writing, production and launch progressed. This was welcome, helpful and typical of the editorial team at Kogan Page, a number of whose members I have worked with in the past.

Introduction

Success is getting what you want.
Happiness is liking what you get.

H Jackson Brown

So you want to succeed in marketing. You are serious about it too
(well, you are reading this!). Good. Marketing is a challenging area
of business, and an exciting and rewarding one in which to work. It
is worth while, too. Marketing is the business function that drives
business, achieves profit and growth – and makes things happen.

Marketing needs all the talent it can get. Can you succeed in the
marketing world? Well, why not? Certainly, if you have the right
characteristics, develop the appropriate skills, obtain the
necessary qualifications, go about things in the right way and…
but we are getting ahead of ourselves. You may just have a germ of
an idea about marketing, you may have short-listed it as one of a
number of possible careers, or you may already be working in it or
near it and wanting to make sure it treats you well. Whatever your
situation, this book is intended to provide practical help.
Specifically, it is designed to:

▌ demystify marketing and explain exactly what it is;
▌ set out the range of career possibilities that exists within it;
▌ give a flavour of what it is actually like to work in marketing;
▌ provide guidelines on the way to proceed to get in, get on – and
  get to the top.

Again, whatever stage you are currently at, it is advantageous to
look ahead – in this case towards a career in marketing – with a
healthy respect for the realities of the world of work as it is now,
and in the light of the trends that will affect it in the future.
Because of this, there are a number of other factors we will touch
on along the way. These include:

▌ deciding what you want from your working life, assessing the situation and matching your needs to the realities of the job market;

▌ active approaches to career development, indeed career management, in a changing world;

▌ focusing on the wide range of opportunities that exists in marketing with a view to short-listing the best area for you and the best career route to take;

▌ looking at the concept of the 'top job' in the context of the span of marketing activity; there are a variety of 'tops' and numbers of ways of getting to them.

The way ahead

The book's organisation reflects these factors. We start in Chapter 1 with an overview and explanation designed to demystify marketing in all its guises. Chapters 2 and 3 review the breadth of opportunities that exists in different job roles and in the marketing of different types of product and service.

We then turn to the jobs involved more specifically: to the range of different jobs it is possible to undertake in marketing (Chapter 4), and the role of the marketing director in Chapter 5. An international flavour is added in Chapter 6 for those who see the world as their market, and then – because it is both topical and important – the area of e-commerce has its own chapter. In Chapter 8, the key skills and qualifications necessary for a marketing career are reviewed.

The final two chapters, Chapters 9 and 10, look at how to plan and manage a career in marketing and where to find marketing jobs; a final reference section adds a variety of names and addresses of useful points of contact (ranging from management institutes to magazines).

Though the objective is to give a full picture of the opportunities in marketing, there is doubtless more to be said. This is not a book about how to undertake marketing and, as will quickly become clear, marketing is a broad subject. Hence, perhaps a final objective is to prompt further investigation; if you are serious about a career in marketing then time spent studying what is involved, how it works and how you can succeed in it is well worth while. This is intended to provide a useful start to that process, with value whatever stage of your career you are at.

This is an objective review. But – let me declare my prejudice – it is one that unashamedly reflects my personal enthusiasm for marketing. I hope that enthusiasm proves infectious, for I do believe that – beyond it being a worthwhile and satisfying area of work – it is also fun. Chapter 1 starts the process and aims to demystify marketing for you.

Patrick Forsyth
Touchstone Training & Consultancy
28 Saltcote Maltings
Maldon
Essex CM9 4QP

Top task boxes

One purpose of this book is to give a flavour not only of what marketing in all its manifestations is, but also what it is like to work in. To this end a number of short, boxed sections appear throughout the text under the heading 'Top tasks'. These give snapshots of some of the tasks that those working in marketing must undertake, and an indication of some of the areas about which you might find questions or discussions focusing in job interviews. The topics chosen range across the main areas of marketing and are not intended to be comprehensive or to put any order of priority on the examples used; they are to add something of a flavour of what working in marketing is all about. They start here.

Top task

How much?

Your product is successful. Its brand name is well known, and it has a hard-won image that adds to its attractiveness for customers. It is a profitable line and its price is carefully

---

matched to its costs, its image and its position in the market-place. Then a new competitor appears. Their product closely matches yours in quality and is currently enjoying a successful launch; it is priced at a lower level than your own product and already there are indications that your sales will be adversely affected.

You must review the relative price of your own product. Should the price be dropped to match or beat the new competitor? Should it be held, or even increased? And what other action must be considered to ensure any threat to your future sales is mitigated?

1 *What is marketing?*

Though much of what is involved in marketing is, to a degree, a matter of common sense, it also involves complexity. For a start, the word marketing is used in (at least) five different ways.

Without a clear overview there is a real danger that consideration of a career in marketing will be stillborn. It is such an overview, setting out the broad picture and demystifying some of the confusion that can surround marketing, that this first chapter briefly describes. Its intention is to allow the reader subsequently to obtain more from a reading of the rest of the book, and to be able to put everything in context.

Scope and definition

Because of the confusion that sometimes surrounds marketing, we will start with a word about what marketing is *not*. It is not a euphemism for advertising, nor a smarter word for selling. Our first objective here is to demystify the word before looking at its relevance and application. Not only is marketing an area in which there is considerable jargon, but the word itself can confuse because there is not just one straightforward definition. It is used in several different ways; and all are broader in scope and complexity than the euphemisms quoted above.

For any business, marketing describes four things:

First, it describes a **concept**. This is the belief that the customer is of prime importance in business, and that success comes from customer orientation – seeing every aspect of the business through the eyes of customers, anticipating their needs and supplying what they want in the way in which they want it, not simply trying to sell whatever we happen to produce. This is surely no more than common sense (though manifestly not something every business embraces in its entirety) and is something that certainly always has relevance. In different businesses, of course, the 'customer' encompasses a number of different people. Goods or services may be sold direct to the public, or to them through others (wholesalers, retailers etc). Other sorts of marketing involve other types of customer, for example business-to-business marketing where, as the words suggest, one organisation is selling to another.

▌ Secondly, marketing describes a **function** of business. To define it formally, it is 'the management function that is responsible for identifying, anticipating and satisfying customer requirements profitably', or in other words it is the process that implements the concept. Such must clearly be directed from a senior level and take a broad view of the business. More simply put, someone must wear the marketing 'hat' (and in so doing must certainly sit in a top job). In smaller companies, this may not be someone labelled 'marketing manager' or whatever: the responsibilities may be with a general manager, sales manager, or promotion manager, or they may be – often are – spread around amongst a number of people. Whoever is involved and however it is arranged, the final responsibility must be clear, and sufficient time must be found to carry out the function.

▌ Thirdly, marketing is an umbrella term for a **range of techniques**; not just selling and advertising but all those techniques concerned in implementing marketing in all its aspects: market research, product development, pricing and all the 'presentational' and promotional techniques including selling, merchandising, direct mail, public relations, sales promotions, advertising and so on.

▌ Fourthly, marketing is an ongoing **process**. This acts to 'bring in the business' by utilising and deploying the various techniques on a continuous basis; and doing so appropriately and creatively to make success more certain. Marketing is not a 'profit panacea'. It cannot guarantee success, nor can it be applied 'by rote' – the skill of those in marketing lies in precisely *how* they act in an area that is rightly sometimes referred to as being as much an art as a science.

So, what does marketing do to achieve its aims and lead an organisation through the potential minefield of external factors that may influence it? A little more about the continuous implementation of the marketing process will help fit the range of techniques into the picture. The implementation, if it is to be successful, must be executed in a way that includes keeping a close eye on external factors. This cycle of activity is shown in Figure 1.1, and starts, unsurprisingly, with the customer. As the process goes on, we can see how some of the classic marketing activities feature and how they relate to the concept in carrying out their own specific role.

First, **market research** attempts to help identify, indeed anticipate, consumer needs: what people want, how they want it supplied and whether they will want it differently in the future. As research can analyse the past and review current attitudes, but not predict the future, it must concentrate on trends, and needs careful interpretation. Even so it can have an important role in reducing risk and assisting innovation. It can be utilised

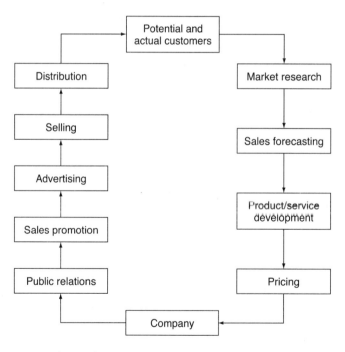

Figure 1.1 The marketing process

throughout the marketing process, and is not just something appropriate at a preliminary stage.

Next, **forecasting** must be used to try to ascertain what quantity of a particular product or service might be purchased in future. Identifying a clear need is of little use commercially if only a handful of people want it. This is typical of areas where marketing does not offer exactitude. Forecasting is not easy – a point well made, albeit in another context, by the physicist Niels Bohr who said, 'Prediction is never easy. Especially of the future.' True enough, forecasting is never 100 per cent accurate, but the best estimate possible needs to be made to aid planning and reduce risk.

Product and/or service development is, for most businesses, a continuous process. Sometimes the process is more evolution than revolution as a product gradually changes. Sometimes it is more cosmetic than real (a new improved floor cleaner with ingredient X); sometimes it is so rapid consumers get upset by the pace of obsolescence – as with computers where it is said that you know that if you have the latest model, it must be obsolete.

No organisation can afford to stand still, and innovation in marketing, rather than the slavish application of the status quo, must be the order of the day.

Price, including all aspects of pricing policy, is normally a marketing variable; price says a great deal about quality – indeed it is an inherent part of a product's image (would you want a cheap Porsche?) – and price levels must be set carefully. This is not only to ensure financial objectives are met, but also to create the appropriate image and feeling of value for money in the market-place. Price is an inherent part of the product or service and must be used as an element of the marketing process.

External communications

With these factors in place, the company must **promote** itself. That is, it must communicate, clearly and persuasively, to tell people what is available and encourage them to buy. A variety of techniques, advertising, direct mail, sales promotion etc, can then be used, together or separately. Of all the promotional tactics, selling is the only personal one. It involves one-to-one communication, and it often forms a final, important link in the chain of different methods that link the company to the market. Thus, in simple terms, promotion creates interest, which sales converts into positive decisions to purchase.

The impact of visibility is clear if you look at the history of many products as they have grown from small beginnings to be market leaders in their field, a process most often driven by the promotional investment made in them.

Lastly, a further important part of marketing, not yet mentioned, is **distribution**. Marketing sometimes involves a direct relationship: you see an advertisement in the newspaper and reply direct to the company; they send you the product. More often there is a chain of intermediaries. Where did you obtain this book? Possibly direct from the publisher, but more likely from a bookshop, or perhaps at a shop in a training, business or educational establishment of some sort. If so, the publisher may have sold it to a wholesaler (or distributor, library supplier etc), which in turn sold it to a bookshop. There is a variety of possible chains that might operate here. A more recent one, of course, involves e-commerce. You might have bought this book from an e-retailer such as Amazon.co.uk, or from the publication _The Good Book Guide_'s Web site. Such situations are duplicated in many industries, so similarly, the new brake light bulb you buy for your car may go from the manufacturer to wholesaler to garage to you; other chains may be longer and there is often both complexity and change with which marketers must contend.

The marketing system

Now all this may well start to make things clearer, but it is still not the complete picture. Lastly, marketing has to operate as a **system** and involves variable factors that operate both inside and outside the marketing organisation. Many of these factors are restrictions. After all, an organisation cannot do just as it wants and ignore the outside world; all sorts of factors, ranging from competitive activity to government action, may conspire to hinder its intentions.

The marketing system links the market (customers and potential customers) with the company, and attempts to reconcile the conflict between the two. A moment's thought will show that the objectives of company and customer are not the same. For example, the organisation may want to sell its products or services for a high profit, whereas the customer wants the best value for money.

There are four elements that comprise the **marketing system**; these position the marketing process within a broader context and link the organisation to the world outside. The four elements are:

1. the market and its segments;
2. the company and its various functions;
3. the marketing mix;
4. the external environment.

We will look here, briefly, at the company situation.

The company and its functions

Every company has three basic functions – though in a well-directed company they do not operate in isolation from one another – and two major resources. The three basic functions are:

▌ production;
▌ finance;
▌ marketing.

The two major resources are: 1) capital; and 2) labour.

Each business function has different tasks and different objectives, often operates on a different time-scale, attracts different types of people and regards money in a different way. So, despite their all contributing towards the same company objectives, there is inevitably internal conflict between, say, marketing and production (and thus the amount of product it is thought should be produced and what may be sold), or between production and finance. (*Note* Organisations do of course vary. 'Production' implies factories and tangible products, but anything has to be produced: for example, software is not really in the same category as, say, a motor car, but it surely has to be produced. Even the team of people who audit a company's accounts represent the production side of the accountancy firm that does the work. So both products and services are involved here.)

If you observe internal friction within any company you may work for currently therefore, relax – that is because you are normal. Table 1.1 shows, in slightly caricatured form, how differences amongst people and functions affect the way things work.

	Finance	Production	Marketing
Objective	to ensure that the return on capital employed will provide security, growth and yield	to optimise cost/output relationships	to maximise profitable sales in the market-place
Time Period of Operation	largely past – analysing results plus some forecasting	largely present – keeping production going, particularly in three-shift working	largely future – because of lead time in reacting to the market-place
Orientation	largely inward – concerned with internal results of the company	largely inward – concerned with factory facilities for personnel	largely outward – concerned with customers, distribution and competition
Attitudes to Money	largely 'debit and credit' – once money is spent, it is gone; money not spent is saved	largely 'cost-effectiveness' – hence value analysis, value analysis techniques and cost cutting	largely 'return on investment' – money 'invested' in promotion to provide 'return' in sales and profits
Personality	often introverted; lengthy training; makes decisions on financially quantifiable grounds	usually qualified in quantitative discipline; makes decisions on input/output basis	often extroverted; sometimes educationally unqualified; has to make some decisions totally qualitatively

Table 1.1 Business functions compared

In many companies subcontracting, for example work done by an advertising agency, is also involved and the activity can spread outside the company itself. Marketing must, therefore, work within the constraints imposed by the way the company functions operationally. Or certainly it must do so to some extent. Profits are, after all, only generated *externally*, and the organisation as a whole must be organised in a way that allows marketing to be market-orientated. The market cares nothing for any internal inconvenience or confusion that may exist. It simply judges a company on its overall external image and the details that contribute to that. Thus things done for internal reasons that do not work in the market may dilute overall marketing effectiveness, and be damaging. Indeed, the 'sales', in say a department store, sometimes offer evidence of marketing people's over-optimism.

The other three elements of the marketing system are sufficiently important to the way things work to deserve their own comment.

Segmentation

This describes the fine detail of markets and how they are subdivided to allow accurate targeting and marketing action. In simple terms marketing activity is directed at segments – portions of the market that are sufficiently homogeneous to have common needs. Thus there is a segment of the motor car market that buys soft-top sports cars, and segments of the detergent market that focus on slightly different things: products that offer economy, or special ability to deal with coloured clothes or biological stains, or that are environmentally friendly and so on. Sometimes such divisions may seem somewhat cosmetic and contrived. On other occasions they define what are essentially separate markets needing different approaches. The distinctions are very real from an operational point of view. (*Note* Another word you will hear used in this way is niche; a niche is essentially only a small, perhaps specialised, segment.)

The marketing mix

This term describes the variables that marketing people must work with in deciding on their chosen strategy. Often referred to as the 'four Ps', these are product, price, place and presentation (the latter encompassing all the promotional and communications techniques from advertising to selling). A variety of different approaches can be taken in each area: one product or a range? High price or low? National or international operation?

Promotion by direct mail or advertising? (Most often a range of different promotional techniques is used, some more than others, and the phrase _communications mix_ or _promotional mix_ is also used.) There are many questions to be addressed here.

The external environment

The external environment is all those factors – including **competition** – that restrict or assist marketing to work. Competition is not simply direct alternatives, for example whether someone buys a Parker pen or a Cross. Competition is wider, with pens competing with pencils, typewriters and word processors – and with CDs, books and socks, as many pens are given as presents. Other external factors affecting marketing can be summarised under four headings:

- _Economic._ Sales are affected by potential customers' ability to buy as well as by marketing; adverse economic conditions may act to stop, delay or change purchasing patterns.
- _Political._ Government can affect things in many ways: a change of safety standards may increase the sales of replacement car tyres; statutory tests make the launch of some products a lengthy business (eg medicines – which cannot be sold until it is clear they will not turn your hair green or make it drop out as well as cure your sore throat).
- _Social._ Social changes continue all the time; consider the many marketing opportunities stemming from more couples with both partners working in recent years (and buying more convenience foods).
- _Environmental._ Many products have a 'green' element to their promotion changing considerations here affect everything from, say, which chemicals can, or cannot, be used in making a product to, for instance, certain cosmetics being promoted as not involving animal testing.

The range of implications stemming from issues falling under these headings is vast. Marketing people cannot operate in a vacuum; they must be aware of a great deal happening around them – indeed they must anticipate changes where possible and certainly respond to them and work with them. Not least, it is here that the search for new opportunities must, in part, take place.

Top tasks
Hello, good evening and...

Your company is in the news. A merger is under way and the new combined company will become a major player in the industry. The press and others tend to focus on the negative sides of such occurrences (witness the volume of coverage in the press about bank branch closures). One product in particular appears to be in direct competition with a similar product – a competitor until the merger. Questions are being asked about how the two products will move forward together, or indeed if one will be axed. You have been invited to be interviewed by a magazine. What you say will be read by customers (and the retailers and others you sell through) and the management and shareholders of both companies, and it will appear at a sensitive time just as the merger is being finalised.

You have to plan what to say. What line will you take? Some decisions are made, and others will follow shortly – how can you avoid giving away plans that would assist competitors, yet reassure customers and others that the whole situation is positive?

Dealing with complexity

Marketing is a complex business – not so much in the sense of being complicated or intellectually taxing to get your head round, but more because there is so much involved. For example:

▍ The *product life cycle* may affect action. Most products are launched, grow and must be taken to a state of maturity, kept there and yet ultimately decline and die. It is a risky business; by no means all new products succeed – and marketing must operate differently at every stage: as products are launched or as action is necessary to revitalise them, for instance. Some have short lives (like a newspaper or pop CD); others are sustained into long, long lives, with brand names like Oxo, Persil and Pears soap having been around for generations.

▌ The power of _intermediaries_ may be of major concern. For example, selling consumer goods to major supermarkets (one of whom might control 25 per cent of the market) needs as much effort and creativity spent on it as does promotion to ultimate consumers.

▌ One company may operate separate, or largely separate, marketing programmes for different products, maybe selling through different outlets for different brands (for example, Seiko and Alba watches).

All this – and much more – extends the variety of jobs in marketing and the variety of tasks each job must cope with; and dynamic markets, fickle customers and predatory competitors make for constant change and a need, whatever else, to be quick on your feet. The variety of opportunities on offer is explored further in the next chapter. First, there are a couple more factors having wide impact on the nature of the marketing process and working in it.

An ongoing process

The whole process, or cycle, of marketing continues all the time, and already we see some of the different facets of marketing falling into place. As we will see, it involves what was referred to earlier as being as much art as science; it is a _creative_ process that has some scientific basis, but no absolute guarantee of success. The customer is always fickle and unpredictable; marketing may be an exciting function of business, but it carries a real element of risk, not least for those working in it. On the other hand, when it goes well it produces considerable satisfaction for everyone involved; this is a stage at which, with a product selling well, the marketing people tend to become convinced that the success is _all_ down to marketing. In fact, as this introduction shows, a wider range of influences is at work. It is because of this that it is often said that everyone in an organisation is involved in marketing. There is a good deal of truth in this. Indeed, it is this need for a wide spectrum of people to be involved that gives rise to the need for what is called a *marketing culture*: a situation where marketing is not just understood around an organisation, but where many others actively contribute to its success. There is a need for an internal as well as an external marketing job to be done in many organisations.

So, marketing is much more than simply a department – or a body of techniques; it is central to the whole reason for an organisation's being and to its relationship with its market and its customers. While, of course, many different activities of a company are important, it is a truism that any kind of organisation can only create profits out in the market. Unless marketing activity, in the fullest sense of the term, creates a situation where customers buy in sufficient quantity, producing the right revenue and doing so at the right time, no business operation will be commercially viable. Marketing has to produce in customers a reason to buy, and make it a more powerful one than any a competitor produces. Whatever the many elements involved, the key is to focus on customer needs and set out to satisfy them at a profit.

Planned activity

One area of marketing immediately explained, notwithstanding the amount of complexity discussed so far, is marketing planning. A key element of the business plan is the marketing dimension. This part of the plan analyses the current situation: a typical method here is the so-called SWOT analysis (an examination of the strengths and weaknesses of the organisation and the opportunities and threats existing in the market-place). It then assesses priorities and options in terms of strategy and sets out an activity plan (what will be done, by whom and when), with links to control and implementation. It provides a 'route map' for operations, a working document both to follow and to use shorter-term to fine-tune approaches selected. Given the investment usually behind the marketing activity of a firm (for example, in research and development, and more), planning is a prerequisite to sensible operational activity. It reduces risk, adds precision and enhances the chances of success.

Top tasks

Plan the work and work the plan

When you joined the company, the lack of any tangible marketing plan made action uncertain and control downright difficult. Rectifying this was a prime task specified by the Board. So, one of your first actions has been to consult widely and draft a clear plan for the next financial year. This has been approved by the Board, along with the financial and budgetary elements that go with it. You now want to use the plan as a communications tool internally to explain, to motivate and specifically to drive the activities of other people – the rest of the marketing team (and beyond).

Soon it must be circulated. How can you ensure a constructive response and make working in a more planned environment acceptable?

Summary

To summarise, and add a note of formality, let me record here that the Chartered Institute of Marketing have an official definition of marketing that reads: 'Marketing is the management process responsible for identifying, anticipating and satisfying customer requirement profitably.' Marketing guru Philip Kotler has defined it by saying: 'Marketing is the business function that identifies current unfulfilled needs and wants, defines and measures their magnitude, determines which target markets the organisation can best serve, and decides on appropriate products, services, and programmes to serve these markets. Thus marketing serves as the link between a society's needs and its pattern of industrial response.'

These definitions certainly express something of the complexity involved. The marketing person who applied the old maxim, 'the most exciting thing you can do with your clothes on', to marketing took a more personal point of view. Certainly, marketing is more than just the 'marketing department'. Another management guru,

Peter Drucker, was content to say simply, 'Marketing is looking at the business through the customers' eyes', and indeed everything stems from exactly that.

The foregoing summarises some key aspects of marketing. You may be at an early stage, where this snapshot simply encourages you to read more. Good idea. There are plenty of books on marketing. One that will fill out the explanation in this chapter and is written to give a sound, straightforward overview to those new to marketing is my own *Everything You Need to Know about Marketing* (Kogan Page) – which has the additional merit of being presented in light-hearted style (see the box, 'Marketing defined', for an example). And, if you want to go further and investigate *how* marketing is undertaken, there is no lack of more detailed texts both on marketing and on individual aspects of it.

Marketing defined

It is said that if a man goes to a party and says to a woman that she needs a man and should come home with him, that's marketing. If he stands on a chair and declares his expertise and availability in matters of love to the assembled company, that's advertising. If he tells one particular woman that he is the world's greatest lover and that she should come home with him, that's selling. And if he is approached by a woman saying that she hears he is the world's greatest lover and asking him to come home with her, then that's public relations. And a good trick for those who can do it. (*Note* In these days of political correctness, it should perhaps be said that the protagonist so described could be of any sexual persuasion.)

With a clear overview of marketing in mind, we can move on to examine the range of career opportunities that marketing presents.

2 The range of opportunities

Opportunities are only opportunities if you know that they exist. In such a broad and disparate field as marketing, there is certainly a danger that a lack of understanding about just how much it encompasses can act to obscure potential opportunities – hence the need to review the field (and to read a book such as this) ahead of making any decisions about whether marketing is the career for you and, if it is, where within it you want to be.

Early on in life, your background and circumstances colour your breadth of vision. One example links two points here. My father was a dentist, a perfectly good and necessary occupation. What is more, it is an occupation that people understand (they may not like it, but they understand it!). All dentists essentially do the same job and fix people's teeth. The first point this high-lights is that this is not the case with marketing; there is no similar easy understanding of it. If something about it intrigues you, you need to find out more, to discover exactly what it in fact entails and where within it you might find a desirable career.

Secondly, your career choice may be influenced by your current knowledge. Brought up in a small town where my father moved primarily in medical and professional circles, I knew little of the business world until the need for career choice prompted some investigation (though I did know I did not want to be a dentist).

Too much choice?

The complex modern world offers many career choices, even though adopting many of them is dependent on acquiring certain skills or qualifications (in my case, even if I could have passed the various qualifications needed to become a dentist, my natural tendency towards hamfistedness would have ruled it out as suitable work). The sheer range of possibilities may make choice difficult. What is needed is a process of narrowing the range of options, focusing on a narrower and narrower list until a final choice becomes clear. Complete career guidance is beyond our brief here. However, once you are at the point of identifying that your future lies in a 'business' career (whether the kind of organisation you see as a potential employer is to be commercial or not), and that marketing is the area you wish to pursue, then the following thoughts may assist your further decision making.

Striking a balance

Any decision to pursue a particular career course needs to incorporate and balance two approaches. The first approach is the *practical*: you need to consider what is possible. In some careers there are basic physical criteria that dictate whether you can go into them. A simple example is being above the minimum height to go into the police. Similarly you need to consider whether it is practical for you to add any abilities a particular course might make necessary, for instance fluency in a foreign language. Practical considerations range wide, from the ease or otherwise of getting into a narrow field of activity, however well suited you are for it, to the working hours that it entails and your ability to work in that way. The second approach is the *desirable*: you need to consider alongside the practical what you really want, and how much you want it. You may be prepared to move heaven and earth to achieve your aims, to set your sights high and to compromise little or not at all.

For most people there must be a degree of compromise – though you should take a considered view of things. Many people manage to get nearer their ideal than they at one time dared to hope – perseverance can be a powerful influence. A practical view is important, but too much compromise might be regretted for a long time. The moral is to balance the two factors very carefully, and set objectives accordingly.

A view of qualifications

For many career choices a formal qualification is simply a necessity. For example, this may be the case in technical fields, where something specific is necessary. For other jobs too a qualification may be necessary – we have all seen job advertisements stating 'graduates only' or similar – but just what the qualification is remains more open. Other career paths are simply made easier to pursue if you are well qualified. Remember, careers are essentially competitive and an employer faced with two similar candidates may make decisions partly on a rule-of-thumb basis – pursuing whoever has the 'best qualifications'. Qualifications are reviewed in more detail in Chapter 8. Here it is only sought to highlight their role in creating opportunities and extending choice.

In this context, certain other points are worth a word or two:

- *Immediate impact*. A qualification may open doors at once, making a particular job application possible soon after the qualification is awarded.
- *Lasting power*. As you move along a particular career path, it can be that the experience you accumulate becomes more important in assisting your progress than an earlier acquired qualification (especially the more general ones). But equally this may not be the case, and you could find yourself blessing the day you completed a course even many years after it was done.
- *Perceptions*. It is worth noting also that a qualification is not always something that produces precise and specific effect – such as an MBA in Marketing scoring nine out of ten, say. The perception others have of what you have achieved is equally important. For example, an employer may be as much impressed by the perseverance shown by your doing something in difficult circumstances as by the qualification it gave you. Or the employer may be influenced by the precise course you opted for and where you went to do it, as much as what it was.

There is, however, a direct relationship between qualifications and the range of options you will be able to consider. It is certainly still

21

possible to succeed somewhere in marketing with little or nothing in the way of formal qualifications, but choice is equally certainly likely to be reduced. Your decisions about what qualifications to take, and when, where and how to undertake them, need considering in this light. As a general rule it is often said that it is better to aim to become well qualified, but there is no one fixed situation to consider here. If you want to be a doctor, say, then certain qualifications are mandatory. Without such a cut-and-dried situation to contemplate, those going into marketing must form a considered view in the light of what they want to achieve in future. We return to this anon.

The marketing process

Even a cursory reading of the first chapter will have given you a flavour of the wide range of jobs to be done in marketing. Although all these fit logically within the overall marketing process, they certainly exhibit differences. Working in public relations, for example, is very different from being a brand manager or being in export. Perhaps one of the things that make marketing an interesting career choice is that it can accommodate a range of different people with different inclinations and skills amongst its many activities.

To provide more detailed and formal examples of jobs within the marketing field I have selected two specific jobs and reproduce here formal job descriptions for each of them. The first provides a brief overview of the core job of marketing manager.

Marketing manager

Description

Responsible for the strategic direction of all marketing activity on specific products/services.

Personal specification

▌ three or more years' experience in marketing, or product management;

▌ able to think strategically and direct delivery;
▌ works well in multi-disciplined teams;
▌ forms close-knit relationships with outside agencies.

Suggested professional qualifications

▌ CIM Postgraduate Diploma in Marketing (DipM);
▌ chartered marketer.

Responsibilities

▌ reports to marketing director;
▌ ensures product/service matches brand positioning;
▌ identifies target markets and works with data manager to provide external agencies with relevant data;
▌ plans communication strategy and liaises with all members of the campaign team to ensure effective and efficient delivery;
▌ analyses results of all marketing activity and presents findings and recommendations to senior management/ product management;
▌ builds close-knit teams, own and cross-departmental;
▌ liaises with external agencies to ensure clear understanding of the marketing strategy.

The above is probably the sort of description that would best fit a largish company, maybe in the fast-moving consumer goods (FMCG) area, which uses outside agencies such as an advertising agency.

The second job description is chosen to represent a more specialised area and is for an agency-based person (ie the description would be a little different for a company that had such a role within its own staff complement).

Research manager – agency

Description

Working in the planning department of an agency, responsible for the delivery of information that will enhance consumer insight.

Personal specification

▌ two or more years' experience; could have started as an executive in an agency or in a specialised research agency;
▌ analytical, and good at interpreting facts;
▌ able to present well, both in writing and face to face;
▌ good interpersonal skills, listens well;
▌ organised, able to get the job done – and see the wood for the trees.

Suggested professional qualifications (CIM)

▌ CIM Postgraduate Diploma in Marketing (DipM).

Responsibilities

▌ work closely with the brand planner and client service team to identify what market information is needed and recommend the best way to get it;
▌ analyse available information and prepare summary reports for planners and client service team;
▌ brief specialist research agencies and work closely with them on delivery;
▌ identify market developments and trends that may have an impact on, or provide an opportunity for, client business. Adopt an international perspective where relevant;
▌ monitor competitor activity, both the agency's and the agency's clients;
▌ as and when required, prepare questionnaires and conduct consumer interviews;
▌ organise all materials required for research purposes;
▌ keep abreast of latest research techniques.

These job descriptions are taken from a publication entitled *The Marketing Workplace: Marketing job descriptions guide*. This is published by the Chartered Institute of Marketing in association with the marketing recruitment agency Stopgap. Available free to members on the CIM Web site, it is also available to others as a monograph (from CIM Direct, tel: 01628 427427). I unhesitatingly recommend it as a useful aid that reviews and explains something of the wide range of career options in marketing. The jobs reviewed in it are listed below:

- account director;
- account executive;
- account manager;
- advertising manager;
- board director – agency;
- board director – client-side;
- brand planner – agency;
- campaign manager;
- communications co-ordinator;
- customer information manager;
- customer relationship manager;
- direct marketing manager;
- events manager;
- group account director – agency;
- internal communications manager;
- marketing director;
- marketing executive;
- marketing manager;
- new media manager;
- online marketing manager;
- partner/alliance manager;
- press officer;
- PR manager;
- product/brand manager;
- promotions manager;
- research manager – agency;
- research manager – client-side.

The themes of variety and range of options in marketing are picked up in Chapters 4 and 5, which aim to give a flavour of what working in some of the main activities of marketing is like. In addition, two further examples from the above list are quoted before the end of the book.

Here, job titles are used in a classic sense. It should be noted, however, that job titles are often used without great precision in the marketing world. 'Marketing manager' is seen as a job title with some status (more so at director level). Thus there is a temptation for the title to be applied to jobs that strictly do not warrant it. Similarly in some organisations there is operational practice that makes identifying true job responsibility difficult. In a small company a general manager may do everything a classic marketing manager would do, and more besides. Elsewhere a marketing manager may be akin to a senior salesperson. Certainly in applying for jobs you should look beyond the title before getting excited.

Top tasks

Tomorrow the world

Your company receives 40 per cent of its revenue from overseas, primarily from Continental Europe. Encouraged by success to date, the board are intent on further overseas growth. But where do you look? Business in Europe has been handled in an essentially hands-on way – distances are manageable; if there is trouble brewing or opportunities to exploit someone can be in Brussels or Frankfurt in a few hours. The board favours South-East Asia as the next target, and is considering opening an office in Singapore or Hong Kong.

You must form a view of the way ahead. Do you go along with the board and aim unquestioningly for the Far East, or do you offer alternatives? What about the need for research and how, precisely, will business be handled at such a distance? The first job may simply be to ask some questions – can you pick the right ones?

A plethora of routes

It is perhaps another attractive feature of marketing that one cannot, in fact, give one clear career pathway for it. There are certainly logical progressions, of course, for instance:

▌ market research, which involves analytical skills, links logically with marketing;

▌ sales can lead to sales management (and may be general or marketing management);

▌ brand or product management is certainly a useful preliminary to full marketing management, and that, in turn, to handling marketing at board level;

▌ strong communications skills are common to a number of areas, such as sales promotion and public relations.

That said, all sorts of routes are possible. Large companies may recruit graduates into a planned traineeship, and put them through a progression that takes in a number of marketing functions, exploring the potential they exhibit in each one before aiming them along a particular path (preferably with their active participation). In other circumstances, progress may happen more from serendipity and planning 'as you go'. For example, computer skills may take someone into the technical side of an IT company, but communications skills, say, may provide the platform for a movement into marketing. Such non-standard progress can be as actively worked at as any other kind.

In all cases, it makes progress more certain if you have clear objectives and aim to manage the development of your career actively – an area investigated further in Chapter 9. I do not want to favour either more conventional or contrived pathways here. Both kinds are possible, though all pathways must be approached practically and need to be worked at if the chances of success are to be increased.

Top tasks

A new broom

Current agreed plans include launching a new product. Product development has gone well and is nearing its end. The next job will be to launch the product on the market. This necessitates considerable promotional expenditure. Because the product will be essentially separate from other marketing activities you have decided to appoint a new advertising agency (while existing elements of your business continue to be handled by the agency now retained for some years and operating successfully on your behalf). The choice of this agency will obviously be pivotal in any success the new product enjoys.

Now you must decide which agency to appoint. How do you brief a short list of agencies as to your requirements? How do you make the final selection?

A basis for decision

By its nature, marketing offers a range of job and career options. A variety of different factors needs to be considered in forming a decision and making a choice. These include:

- you – your character, likes, dislikes, skills and qualifications;
- the functional area of marketing you see as attractive (eg PR or advertising);
- the actual job you want to do (eg sales manager or market researcher);
- the product or service an organisation markets (and thus the industry it is within);
- the size, and thus nature, of organisation that will be your employer;
- the markets you will be involved in (eg industrial or consumer, national or international).

There is a good deal to contemplate; an informed and considered decision is usually best, and these areas of decision and more are touched on in the remaining pages.

One thing should be clear at this stage: not only does the world of marketing offer an interesting, exciting and worthwhile career choice, but it can appeal to a wide spectrum of people because of the plethora of different job choices it offers. There is certainly no lack of opportunities for anyone suitable looking at the marketing area; indeed many would say that marketing needs all the talent it can attract. We continue our explanation of marketing, and turn in the next chapter to the many things marketed. Choice here will affect careers and the work done during them.

A final question – rewards

Before we move on from a review of the opportunities marketing offers it is perhaps a good idea to address the question of rewards (unless you seek no remuneration for your work!).

Clearly pay varies depending on a number of factors such as size of employer and the precise role within marketing that a job entails. Someone in a top job in a specialised area such as market research, for instance, might well earn more than a marketing manager in certain kinds of organisation, for example a smaller firm. Given the range and scope of marketing there is some complexity in comparisons. Any specific figures quoted would, of course, quickly date.

However, overall salaries do compare well with other jobs in the organisational world. They are well documented too, so at any particular time you can get an overview of the state of play – perhaps the state of pay. The main survey to check is _The Marketing Rewards Survey_ compiled annually by the Chartered Institute of Marketing (in association with the Rewards Group). This is available for purchase, though it is quite expensive. You may find a copy of it in a business library, or the summary published in the Institute's magazine _Marketing Business_ may give you sufficient information.

Without going into specific figures it may be worth noting that the remuneration for marketing jobs:

▌ has recently been increasing ahead of inflation;
▌ at senior level is ahead of other main organisational functions (including finance, computing and human resources), though at mid-level this is not true;
▌ is normally higher in organisations with high turnover than in those with lower turnover;
▌ includes some sort of bonus or incentive payment – this is pretty much the norm for marketing staff, with the most senior people getting the greatest bonuses;

▌ varies a little with regard to gender: men in marketing seem to earn more than women, with the gap being greatest at the most senior level;

▌ includes, for most marketing people, a company car as part of their package (though the exact policy about this is more volatile of late, given constant changes in government policy about the tax that company cars attract).

As with any job, the careerist should be as much concerned about the package as the immediate salary. If you are young, do not ignore things like pensions (they will matter soon enough!). Remember too that marketing is more likely to involve rewards that link to results than many other aspects of business, and that some of these may come in the form of things like share options that do not pay the mortgage from day one, but which can be worth a significant amount in the longer term.

Marketing has much to offer, and that includes the financial return as well as the satisfactions. With that in mind we turn to further factors affecting choice of marketing career; first we consider what is marketed.

3 *Marketing what?*

Marketing is concerned with getting goods and services to the market-place; and with making a profit in the process. As such those in marketing have to market... well, something. There are those who say that marketing is a generic skill, that if you can market one thing successfully, then you can market anything – well, perhaps practically anything. I am reminded of the cracks about 'not selling refrigerators to Eskimos' (although they do indeed need refrigerators, not to keep their food cold but to keep it warm enough to cook without defrosting – sorry, I digress). Certainly there are plenty of choices about what product or service to get involved with in terms of its marketing.

Whatever the truth about marketing being a generic skill – and some product areas are surely specialised and need special skills – what you market certainly affects the job of marketing it. Some fields may be good stepping-stones (we return to this) and that alone may have merit. Otherwise you need to consider how the nature of marketing in different fields varies and how each would suit you.

For the most part the consideration, and the focus of this chapter, hangs around the product or service involved. After all, there is all the difference in the world between toothpaste and, say, ball bearings (which would crack your teeth even if you could get them to stay on the toothbrush!). There are, more seriously, big differences in their marketing and in the jobs of so doing. But there are other factors to bear in mind, albeit they link to what is being marketed. Some of the other factors you might want to bear in mind include:

▌ *Location.* The location that you work in obviously affects life-style. It may or may not be important to you. Some sorts of company cluster in particular locations. For example, pharmaceutical firms seem predominantly to be in the south-east of England, many financial institutions are in the City of London, most china producers are in the Potteries, retailers are in high streets and shopping centres, and those catering for the agricultural market tend not to be found in cities. This is perhaps something about which you should take both a short- and long-term view; a location you favour now may be different from one that suits if you have a young family to bring up. Many aspects of location are important, even for example the fact that in a central location to which people commute there may be little social contact amongst staff who could live far apart in opposite directions.

Breadth of operations. This too will affect location. A company involved in or intent on a purely regional role will usually locate in that region. Size may also affect the resources and budgets they have available (including the budget for staff), and the scope of jobs may be limited by comparison with a larger and more broadly based concern.

International involvement. If you want to travel or relocate abroad on either a temporary or permanent basis, then you really have to aim ultimately to work for a firm that is, in some way, involved internationally. If you speak a second language, that may be an asset, but might also limit potential travel to areas where that language is spoken. Maybe your ambitions can only be realised by learning another language.

People. Work involves you with people: colleagues, staff and, in marketing, customers. Some people you like and some you do not; some you hate. While you do not have to like everyone at work sufficiently to want them to come to dinner, say, there could be certain kinds of people with whom you would prefer not to work. This is not intended to be censorious. It is just a fact of life that most of us get on better with some kinds of people than others. You may want to avoid being tainted by the grey of accountants; you may want to select an environment where the majority of people will be women, or men. Another aspect of this is age. Do you want to work with a group of people who are predominantly your own sort of age? All such factors are considerations, and there are choices to be made about what will and will not suit you in this regard.

Level of pay. Some industries pay better than others. Which they are depends on the current situation and changes over time.

The information technology industries have been paying well of late, but could be eclipsed by something else. I began my career in publishing, renowned then and now for being a poor payer; I might still be in it if plans to marry had not necessitated my earning more money. The size of organisation might also have a bearing, as might its being in the private or public sector.

▌ _Fit with temperament or skills._ Clearly there has to be a fit here. High-tech industries are not for those with no computer skills and no interest in such things. Jobs that rely on the written word a lot will not attract those who cannot write three consecutive words in a logical order for a written report. A creative streak might attract you to an advertising agency or a firm selling fashion products.

▌ _Level of risk._ This links again to your temperament. While industry, as the introduction made clear, does not offer the wholly safe career paths it used to do, some fields are inherently more risky than others. Some organisations too have particular attitudes to this, like the US firm that said it operated a policy of 'planned insecurity', explaining that it fired whoever was bottom of the sales league every month. Some people thrive in this sort of environment, but not, of course, all.

▌ _Culture._ This is an important one. There is culture in the sense of purpose. You may prefer to work for an organisation that 'does something worthwhile', however you define that. It might mean a charity (they are big business these days), or a health care operation. There is also culture in the sense of atmosphere and the kind of people who work there: I imagine there is all the difference in the world between working for, say, the Disney organisation and working for a shipbuilding company.

▌ _Ethical considerations._ You may not want to flood the world with military equipment (or toilet cleaner either if it is going to kill every fish within a hundred miles of customers' drains). This is an area of serious thinking for some.

These are certainly areas for decision. Realistically most people are conscious of their choice involving a degree of compromise. So be it. At least you need to think the issues through and make a decision that you can live with and one that is most likely to give you what you want.

Next we will examine some main divisions, putting potential employers into major camps with their different characteristics. We will also define some of the jargon that seems to pervade the world of marketing.

Top tasks
On display

Your product sells through a variety of major stores. All the product range is attractively boxed and this enhances its appearance on display. Because the product range is varied, boxes vary in size, as do prices and margins. Your customers – the stores – allocate you shelf space but this is rarely sufficient to display your full product range. In addition, some products sell faster than others and stock needs to replace these fast. Gaps on the shelf quickly get taken up, often by competing products, and sales are then lost.

You need to supply exactly the right mix of products to maximise sales. How can you calculate the mix of products, box sizes, price, margin and varying rate turnover to produce a basis for selling in the right mix? And in so doing can you make the procedure you then use acceptable and attractive to the retailers?

Consumer, industrial, business-to-business or service product marketing

Consumer goods

First we will consider the marketing of what are called consumer goods. Let us be clear first what this terminology means. Consumers are customers in the sense of the public – you and me – going to the shops. The core area of consumer products is referred to as FMCGs (fast-moving consumer goods) – those things that turn over fast because consumers want to make routine purchases (household products like soap and toothpaste that are bought regularly). I once heard the marketing director of the division of ICI that makes shotgun cartridges speak at a conference. He began by saying that his product was the fastest moving in the room! Maybe stretching the sense a little.

Consumer product marketing is perhaps the high-profile end of marketing. It is what many people think of when the word marketing is mentioned. It is characterised by being:

- very visible – these are products seen everywhere;
- directed at large markets – everyone is a customer for tooth-paste (well, except maybe the guy who sits next to you on the bus);
- promoted in many media – from television advertising to advertisements in glossy magazines;
- backed by large budgets, especially for promotion – which are necessary to reach the large markets, and do so repeatedly;
- highly competitive – in many product areas there are many companies making essentially similar products;
- reliant on the creation of 'brand image' – the product name (and the whole 'personality' that goes with it);
- creative in approach – witness the style of many consumer advertisements (though these may well be originated by the advertising agencies much used in this sector to plan and organise the promotional campaigns).

In consumer marketing many of the large firms have a string of brand names; and all need marketing. Sometimes this is apparent, as with the many products marketed under, say, the Nestlé name. Other companies use a list of different brand names and the association with the main company is not featured strongly (as with Lever Brothers). Multiple brands and wide product ranges give rise to the job of **product manager** (sometimes called brand manager), essentially someone who acts as 'mini-marketing manager' for a single brand rather than a whole organisation. Given the scale of marketing in this field, it is a big job, and the task of achieving the planned **market share** (the percentage of total sales of similar products) is a challenge. This is a favoured career path for many people.

So, life spent marketing consumer goods is certainly in the heartland of the marketing world. Opinions differ. Some people feel that this is the only real marketing. Certainly it is a sophisticated form, one that utilises the full panoply of marketing techniques. Others, for whom the subject of marketing activity is important, feel that the product areas involved are not the most interesting. It is worth thinking this through. You may not instinctively feel that helping sell, say, washing-up liquid is your life's work, but do not overlook the fact that the competitive pressures and challenge of making anything successful in the market-place are just as real whatever the product.

Top tasks

Customer pressure

You are responsible for the marketing of a recently launched FMCG food product. The launch went well and sales are on target. One of the major supermarket groups is asking to see you. So far they have accounted for 26 per cent of your sales and are, by any definition, a major customer. You want sales through their outlets to continue and to grow. You have future promotional plans that need implementation throughout the trade if sales are to be maintained and grow, so you need their support. Yet you are conscious that they are effectively very powerful (at worst, if they stopped stocking your product, 26 per cent of sales go out the window).

You have to plan for an important meeting. What do they want? How can your negotiating skills ensure that you maintain good relations with them without sacrificing profitability?

Industrial products

Industrial products tend to be a very different area of marketing, that of 'heavy' goods sold to industry rather than goods sold to 'Joe Public'. Again the range is considerable. It includes engineering products such as machine tools and related items (from spare parts to specialised oil); complex items such as ships and space shuttles; and a mass of products necessitated by what is called **derived demand**. (For example, a company might manufacture and sell bottles, which are bought by a brewery and filled with beer. The success of the beer in the market dictates how many bottles are sold, but the design of the bottle may be such that it helps produce an attractive image and sell the beer. Wheels within wheels. Cheers.)

There is some variety here, but industrial product marketing is characterised as follows:

▌ There is an inherently smaller number of potential customers – everyone may need toothpaste, but I for one do not have or want an industrial lathe in the back bedroom.

▌ It often involves long lead times as products are designed and engineered – a new car may take four or five years to produce, and a new airliner twice that time.

▌ It usually addresses professional buyers – people paid to buy and trained to get the deal they want.

▌ The people working in it will perhaps need a technical background, qualification or understanding – this will vary of course but can be extreme (the lowest form of life in some marketing departments has a PhD in nuclear physics). There are plenty of opportunities in marketing for those with specialist technical knowledge or qualifications.

▌ It has more specialist and targeted approaches – it is wasteful to advertise, say, heat exchangers on television, but advertisements in technical journals still need to do an effective job.

▌ Personal selling may have a more important role – the final link in the chain is often a personal contact.

Marketing is just as necessary in these areas, and for those with a technical bent the product areas involved may be inherently more interesting. The choice is wide.

Industrial marketing and the next category, business-to-business marketing, are not precisely separated. There is an overlap.

Business-to-business products

These have much in common with industrial products. The term business-to-business, which is how industrial products are sold, is self-apparent and came into use as a phrase more recently than industrial marketing. The difference is primarily that business-to-business omits the heavy end of industrial marketing.

The products here are those bought by offices, factories and what has recently become know as the SOHO market (small office/home office). They include a vast range of things. To illustrate, the following is a pure miscellany by way of example: telephones (and telephone systems), office furniture, paperclips, computer disks, technical journals, stationery, business books and cupboards (on the basis that even the business that has everything needs somewhere to keep it!). There is a further overlap with computers, software and other high-tech product areas mentioned later in this chapter. Essentially all the products a business must buy to keep itself and its people in business are included.

Brands are as important here as in the consumer market; indeed some brand names appear directed at both (you may see a Mercedes car as an attractive prestige product, and then find a dirty delivery van outside your door with the same logo on the bonnet). Here again the career choice is considerable, and the relationship with your own attitudes and interests important.

But there is another category that is important, and again there is an overlap with what has been mentioned already – not all products are products.

Services

Some products are services. These may be sold to the consumer sector, like dry cleaning, tax-free savings accounts and film processing; or to business and industry, like industrial design, contract ploughing and staff training; or to both, like accountancy, insurance and travel. Again you will find a moment's thought shows that there are many examples. How is service marketing different?

▌ Services are intangible – the fact that they cannot be tested by potential customers in advance of purchase in the same way as a product can certainly makes for a different approach to marketing and selling.

- Services are inextricably bound up with service – they are the 'people businesses', and marketing and the organisation of delivery of the service overlap.
- Services interface very directly with customers – much more closely than in some other businesses.
- Services allow change and flexibility to be greater, and sometimes easier, than in other kinds of business (producing a new insurance policy, say, is inherently easier than producing a new jet fighter).

The immediacy of services appeals to some people more than others. It is also worth bearing in mind the way in which services have grown in importance in recent years. This is especially so in countries like the United Kingdom that have seen their manufacturing base decline.

Having defined things to this extent, and with some overlap continuing, we can look at two further 'sectors' affording career choice (and then, briefly, at a number of specialist industries).

Social marketing

This phrase describes what has become a major force in the marketing world. Marketing traditionally described effort designed to produce profit. But not every organisation is profit-making. Well, some, it must be said, fail to make a profit despite their best efforts, but here I am identifying those that do not want to make a profit. It should be remembered that only the tiniest amount of money makes the difference between breaking even and making a profit or loss; in other words, achieving whatever financial out-turn may be required needs some skill. There are three main sectors:

- _Charities_. These days many charities are, by any definition, big business. Their target market is contacted to produce funds, and marketing methods may be used in different ways (to change public or government attitudes, for instance), but marketing is real and important for them and they need marketing talent to achieve their aims and fulfil their charitable purposes. Such organisations are an interesting option for some of those wanting to pursue a career in marketing.

▌ *Government*. Both local and national government have marketing operations. These may be on a grand scale, as with advertising to highlight the dangers of drinking and driving, or to communicate the need to adjust to self-assessment taxation systems; or less major and more local, as with local authority schemes to help small business. Sometimes the target of such marketing is more bizarre. In Singapore, where I work regularly, the government messages are much in evidence. At one time, when population increase was seen as being desirable, television advertising called for people to fall in love. I contemplated writing in to say my visit was only four or five days but I would do my best, but felt the relevant ministry would probably not see the funny side of it. Overall, there are significant and interesting opportunities here for some in marketing.

▌ *Quasi-government and others*. The government category overlaps with this one, which includes a whole range of other bodies: government agencies, trade organisations (like the Wool Marketing Board), educational establishments and professional bodies (such as the Institute of Chartered Accountants, which promotes the merits of working only with an appropriately qualified accountant). Again marketing is much in evidence, and career opportunities exist for those who see this sector as interesting or worth while.

Another sector also offers specialist possibilities.

Marketing services

A plethora of specialist services exist in marketing: advertising agencies, which create advertising for their clients and are specialists in selecting appropriate media; subsectors of this, for example agencies specialising in sales or point-of-sale promotion; and market research agencies, which conduct surveys to identify markets, test products and try to reduce the risk inherent in the marketing process.

More specialist agencies still are concerned with packaging design, photography or copy-writing. All have opportunities for people wanting to work in one specialised sector of marketing. All such agencies have to market their own services too, so there are jobs that let you wear the marketing hat as well as those for people wanting to deploy specialist skills.

Beyond that there is the question of industry specialisation.

Industry specialisation

Of course industries differ, and part of the choice in careers in the commercial world generally hangs around this and how individuals see themselves. Some industries are very specialised (not so much technically, but in ways that affect their marketing and the people who undertake it). The following are mentioned by way of example, but it may be worth examining others for similar sorts of factors.

▌ _High tech and information technology_. The world of computers, the Internet and high-tech products, for both consumers and industry, is certainly specialised. It can be high-risk, and change can occur radically and rapidly (for how long after fax machines arrived would you have wanted to work for a company making telexes, and how long will we see fax machines continue selling now e-mail has become so well established?). Companies in this sector are often internationally based; many are foreign-owned. This is the sort of challenging environment that appeals to many people. It tends (it is difficult to be definitive about such an area) to consist of organisations that employ younger people, that are less formal than many and that expect a lot in return for the higher-than-average remuneration they often pay. It is a field in which you would expect to move job more often than in some others. But it is certainly a driving force in modern industry and worth a look for many.

▌ _Professional services_. This phrase encompasses a clutch of businesses that sell their expertise. Principally, they consist of those that consider the word 'profession' is spelt with a capital 'P' and demand qualifications of their professionals. They include accountants, lawyers, surveyors and architects. It is a category that is usually broadened to include a range of consultants (from consulting engineers to executive recruiters), property firms and

41

more. It has a good deal in common with business services such as market research and an overlap with financial services. This is an area that, in terms of marketing, has changed radically in the past several years, going from an environment of low competition and little marketing to fierce competition and increasingly sophisticated marketing. Initially, with few if any people around with experience of the sector, professional services imported marketing people from other industries. Now there are many firms in this sector and a strong demand for good marketing people. Jobs can involve a considerable amount of internal marketing to carry professional staff along and ensure their involvement. There are some big businesses in this sector; for instance, a firm like PricewaterhouseCoopers – accountants and consultants – employs many thousands of people and has offices throughout the world. You may feel it is a sector worth a look. As an example of an industry undergoing changes that create special opportunities it is worth mentioning (you can read more about this kind of marketing in my book *Marketing Professional Services*, published by Kogan Page).

Pharmaceuticals. The companies that research, create, test and then market drugs and associated products to the medical world are certainly a special category. There are mainly a few large players in this market. Most are international companies. This field is heavily regulated (and quite right too, say I – I do not want to grow scales after taking a cough medicine). They are competitive, but also profitable – discover and patent a cure for some major nasty and the money will roll in for years. Well, I simplify – everything needs marketing and the job of selling to doctors and hospitals is a challenging one. There are products too that require no prescription (OTC or over-the-counter medicines), and these are akin to FMCG products in the way they are marketed. This is an example of an industry that is more exclusive – its marketing people are expected to have experience of it and people move between industries less often. Although it is no less commercial than many others, some people like this sort of field because it is inherently worth while. And, let us be honest, some products are pretty frivolous – for instance, did you know that there is a Japanese washing-up liquid that is wholly intended for washing fruit with before eating it? Really.

▌ *Financial services.* Everyone loves to hate the banks, and this sector contains much more than the traditional banking organisations. If you feel that money makes the world go round then you may consider that this might be an industry to become involved with. Again there are many changes in train. Branches are closing, postal and telephone accounts reign supreme and Internet accounts are growing apace (although as I write it still seems a little easy for the average hacker to siphon money out of them!). A suitable element of service must remain, and customers want to have trust in financial institutions. Such an industry spans the old and the new. Make no mistake, much about it is very traditional (and by some standards slow-moving) but changes will doubtless continue and it will be largely the marketing people who make them happen. You could be one of them.

There is no space here to review every industry. Many have particular, and sometimes topical, characteristics that make them a good fit for some people. Industry is not the only differentiating feature of potential employers, however, so on to another.

Fishes and ponds

A prime difference that occurs in the circumstances in which different people find themselves working relates to the size of their employer. Some organisations are big. Some are not. Bigger may not just mean larger; it can mean different. A large organisation may:

▌ pay better;
▌ provide internal prospects of advancement;
▌ have greater resources (of all sorts);
▌ produce a more social environment (there are probably more people – that's a start);
▌ look better on your CV in terms of the impressiveness or otherwise of your career record.

In addition, marketing jobs in larger companies may be themselves 'larger', having greater responsibility and scope. A top job in such a company may be high-profile within an industry, especially if it involves a brand leader. Or, of course, this may not be true. Large firms vary, as do all.

There are those people whose job in a smaller organisation exhibits all, or most, of these characteristics. Some find the more manageable environment of a small organisation more amenable. There is a choice to be made: do you prefer to be a big fish in a small pond or a small fish in a bigger pond – or a big fish in a big pond?

Because of the nature of marketing, particularly of its more creative aspects, there are no rules here. People travel many routes to success; and some travel (move from employer to employer) more or less than others too. What suits you is not least in importance, and it would be profoundly unsatisfying to spend long in any kind of organisation with which you just did not fit or with which you did not have sympathy, however successfully you might perform in it.

A sure route to the top

The one sure way to the top job in a company is to start (or take over, I guess) the company. I took that route, moving from being a director of a company with over a hundred professional consultancy staff to setting up my own enterprise. I have enjoyed both aspects of my career. My firm may be small, but it is mine! Seriously, considering such options makes the variety of marketing careers clear. In a small firm – whether it is your own or not – all the administrative things that you take for granted in a big company suddenly come into sharp focus. Want something to go in the post? Then you walk to the post-box. But control is absolute, and being able to do what you want is very much part of some people's brief for a good work situation. For example, latterly in my old company my work in Singapore was sometimes regarded as a distraction taking me away from the main work scenario. I like that part of the world and made an effort to maintain the continuity. Now, since I have been the boss, I do not think there has been a word of criticism about my trips – not even once! And they fit well with other things to create the work pattern I want (a little of this book was typed on a laptop sitting by a hotel swimming pool in Singapore!).

Starting your own business is an option in a marketing career. It certainly jumps you to the top, and puts a wide range of responsibilities on your shoulders, all of which must go well if the business is to flourish. Many small businesses, perhaps founded by someone with great competence in whatever the firm does (graphic design, say), founder through lack of marketing expertise. So, if you can find the right business, you may have a head start. Experience may be necessary (except, if you believe the hype, in e-commerce) so it may not be something to do at once. But it is an option.

An opportunity

It should be regarded as a strength of marketing as a career choice that it offers so many options (and there are more to come in Chapter 4). I make no apologies for this chapter not providing a clear and infallible way of making definitive choices; that is the nature of the beast. But choices do need to be made, and it has been the intention here to provide guidance on the criteria you personally need to keep in mind as you make them.

Career structures in marketing are not especially rigid. You may well be able to change, moving from, say, a small company to a larger one, switching industry or whatever. Indeed this can happen several times. You should always remember though that we all spend a long time at work over a lifetime. Making the choice to go into marketing is important; selecting the theatre of marketing in which you want to work is important too. Think carefully. Then aim for what you think suits you best; aim high and go for it.

4 *Working under the marketing umbrella*

Marketing may be a fascinating and challenging area in which to work, and the range of opportunities may be legion, but what exactly, you may ask, do you actually do? In this chapter we investigate some of the main elements of marketing a little more, both to explain them and to give a flavour of the work that takes place in each area. This, alongside what was said in Chapter 3, fills out the criteria for career choice.

The headings here follow the sequence used in describing the marketing process in Chapter 1 and it may be useful to keep this in mind, especially if you are not yet much involved in marketing.

We begin, as anything about marketing should, with customers – and finding out what they might want.

Market research

There is more to research than the lady with the clipboard by whom you may sometimes have been stopped in the street. She has a marketing job, though not perhaps a top one – whoever organises that kind of research, however, may well have a senior job. But we are getting ahead of ourselves; not only is market research an area with its own techniques and technicalities, but it has to relate to overall marketing activity, particularly in planning and decision making. Its key purpose might be summarised as acting to produce the information necessary to make taking sound marketing decisions possible – and reduce the risk they entail.

To help define the terms involved, and make clear the purpose of research in this context, the following is quoted from the book, *The Effective Use of Market Research* (Kogan Page). This was written by Robin Birn, with whom I have worked in association regularly over some years, and who runs Strategy, Research and Action Ltd. It is an excellent reference – now in paperback – for anyone who wants to know more about this area.

> Decision making is central to carrying out managerial functions to make the planning and monitoring process work. Good decisions are taken on the basis of availability and use of relevant information. The information of most concern to marketing management comes from markets and customers, present, potential and future, and concerns the shape, size, nature, needs, opportunities and threats within the market. Market research is the means of providing them with that information.

Definition of market research

The traditional definition of market research is: 'The systematic problem analysis, model building and fact finding for the purpose of improved decision making and control in the marketing of goods and services.'

This implies that research is not just an information tool but a means of providing guidance to help improve the abilities of management within an organisation, as well as a means of making a contribution to the management of the marketing mix. It can be used to help decide on: the marketing strategy required to meet the challenge of new opportunities; the market gaps to approach; and the key areas of interest for future marketing strategies.

Purposes of market research

The two essential purposes of research are: 1) to reduce uncertainty when plans are being made, whether these relate to the marketing operation as a whole or to individual components of the marketing mix such as advertising or sales promotion; and 2) to monitor performance after the plans have been put into operation. In fact, the monitoring role has two specific functions: it helps to control the execution of the company's operational plan and it makes a substantial contribution to long-term strategic planning.

Simply stated, research covers all the 'finding out' activities of marketing. It is the essential first stage of a marketing function – the identification of consumer needs. It describes five major types of research:

▌ *market research* – who buys what and in what quantity (the term market research also acts as an umbrella term for this list; note particularly the difference between market research and marketing research);

▌ *product research* – what is right and wrong with the products of the company, or part of them;

▌ *marketing research* – research into marketing methods: are we communicating and distributing effectively?

▌ *motivational research* – why people buy the products they do and what they feel about them;

▌ *attitude surveys* – customers' attitudes to the products and to the companies that make them.

Like any other form of research, market research can only investigate past behaviour. This is of course very helpful in predicting future behaviour, but research as such cannot be conducted on the future. When attempts are made (opinion polling, intention surveys etc), then serious errors can be made – you may remember some at election time.

The role of research, therefore, is to improve the basis of fact on which forecasts and decisions are made. The difference between researching the past and predicting the future must be clearly recognised.

Top tasks

Finding out

You work for a major professional service organisation, having joined recently to help them accelerate their growth plans through better marketing. Though successful, the firm has grown on a rather *ad hoc* basis. Clients clearly like the way their work is done, but it is less clear why they choose the firm in the first place. As growth requires increased promotion it is important to know who this should be directed at, both in terms of target markets and the level of decision-maker. New promotion must also extend and build on (and possibly correct) the existing perceptions of the firm. Again it is unclear precisely what perceptions there are amongst clients and others in the market-place.

You need to find out, to create a foundation of fact from which to operate. To do so needs research, something designed to produce an objective and accurate view of current market perceptions. How do you decide a precise brief for and set up such a project? And how do you organise to use the findings constructively to change the way the firm operates and the attitudes of many of its professional staff?

The role of market research

It is worth spelling out in a little more detail the range involved here. Market research provides information that assists an organisation to define opportunities for product development and market strategy. It works by assessing whether marketing strategies are well targeted, and identifying market opportunities or changes that are required by customers. Market research tends to confirm issues that are well known in a market initially, but if planned well and effectively it will also identify new opportunities, market niches or ways by which to improve sales, marketing and communications activities.

The role of market research, therefore, and the people in it, is to reduce uncertainty in decision making, monitor the effects of decisions taken and identify the performance of a company or a product in the market.

To be more specific, we can list five key uses for market research:

▪ to identify the size, shape and nature of a market, so as to understand the market and marketing opportunities;
▪ to investigate the strengths and weaknesses of competitive products and the level of trade support a company enjoys;
▪ to test out strategic and product ideas that help to define the most effective customer-led strategies;

▌ to monitor the effectiveness of strategies;
▌ to help to define when marketing expenditure, promotions and
   targeting need to be adjusted or improved.

The variety of purpose here makes it clear that market research is
not simply a 'first check'. It is useful ahead of any action, but it also
provides a means of checking and refining as operations proceed.
Companies that have selected one of these uses for market
research, especially if they have tight budgets, are concerned to
make the research a worthwhile investment. Best results come
when their marketing and sales planning is influenced by the
results.

To illustrate further, some of the main reasons for using market
research are as follows:

▌ to provide data on the market, or a market segment, and to
   discover whether the sector is increasing, staying the same or
   decreasing in importance to customers;
▌ to obtain information to help to understand who the customers
   are, and the way in which they buy and use certain products;
▌ to evaluate customer service, assessing what customers feel
   about the services they are receiving;
▌ to research customer attitudes and needs on a continuous basis
   to know which product types are selling and where there are
   opportunities for new sales;
▌ to achieve better targeting, understanding what media and
   messages influence consumers to buy the products;
▌ to identify changes in the market that will affect how marketing
   must proceed in future.

Sources of information

This also is an important area. Sources include:

▌ *internal records* – a prime source, which when processed can
   reveal much about the characteristics of customers, what they
   buy and how;
▌ *published information* – from whatever source;
▌ *field survey* – should only be used when the first two sources are
   exhausted, or surveys will be conducted that simply discover
   (very expensively) what is already known.

Research techniques

Here the work includes:

- *Sampling*. In most markets, to contain the research within practical limits sampling must be used. It uses probability theory to predict the characteristics of a total universe from a small section within definable limits. The commonest sampling methods are random and quota, particularly the latter as it is cheaper to implement.
- *The questionnaire*. This must be carefully designed to ensure the forming of the questions does not bias the answer.
- *Research methods*. Questionnaires can be administered in person, on the telephone, or by post. There is an inverse correlation between accuracy and cost. In certain types of research, eg motivational studies, group interviews are often used.

Running a research project

Management must first decide as precisely as possible what it wishes to know. To ask for 'everything about the market' is very expensive and often unusable.

Secondly, it must be decided whether to use internal staff (either researchers or other personnel, eg the sales force) or an outside agency. When the costs and possible prejudices of internal staff are considered, it is often at least equally economic to use specialists.

The project brief and method must be clearly defined, and acceptable tolerances and timings set. If outsiders are being used, several proposals should be sought to ensure the fullest possible exploration of the problem. When the findings are available, they should be checked against any other data, and an action programme of decisions drawn up based on the facts identified. Otherwise, although very interesting, the survey will become yet another item clogging the filing system.

The value of research

For research to give the value it should, management must answer the following questions:

▌ What decisions do we have to make?
▌ When?
▌ On what information will they be based?
▌ How accurate does the information need to be?
▌ How quickly do we need it?

No company can risk operating without research, even though the 'research' is purely deep experience of company staff. As decisions get bigger, however, it is worth the insurance of real research to establish a better fact basis.

To conclude I will quote Robin Birn again, from the book mentioned earlier in this chapter. He describes the results of using research as a 'win–win' situation, and defines it so neatly it seems unfair to paraphrase the thought.

> Using research is a 'win–win' situation for those who interpret it and action it effectively. Management wins first time when the research confirms its prejudices, ideas and experiences so providing reassurances that it is taking the right decisions. It wins a second time if the research provides new information or gives a new focus or emphasis on the subject being researched.
>
> Over a period of time users of research also find that they win a third time. If they take a step back to look at the original findings of the research objectively then they can design more interesting and more relevant research than had been completed originally. Research therefore helps management to win by indicating the action it needs to take.

For all its strengths it must never be forgotten that research can only ever provide part of the answer, particularly when decisions are required affecting future action. Judgement (and experience) must always go hand in hand with research, and exercising judgement is something else marketing people must do.

Job implications

The detail given here shows the importance and complexity of research. It demands of those in it a series of particular skills such as questionnaire design, sampling and statistical analysis, and report writing. Overseeing the process is a senior level responsibility; certainly the interpretation of research findings demands a good knowledge of marketing overall.

Market research provides two routes for job seekers. First, there is the agency route. Market research is often subcontracted. Market research agencies can be big businesses in their own right and provide jobs at every level. The people in the agency who head up the client link with major client companies themselves have significant jobs. Second, there is the company route. Large companies may have their own departments to conduct continuing research; the heads of such sections might well be regarded as having top jobs.

The plethora of jobs in the specialist areas of research can all provide possible starting-points to a marketing career that progresses beyond this specialist area. And senior research jobs are themselves amongst the range of marketing top jobs.

Advertising

Now we turn to the 'visible' bit of marketing – advertising – something we see all around us day by day. First a definition: advertising is 'any paid form of non-personal communication directed at target audiences through various media in order to present and promote products, services and ideas'. More simply, it can be called 'salesmanship in print or film'. As with research, there are jobs here in both agencies and companies. The role of advertising, as one of a number of variable elements in the communication mix, is 'to sell or assist the sale of the maximum amount of the product, for the minimum cost outlay'.

There is a variety of forms of advertising, depending upon the role it is called upon to play among the other marketing techniques employed, in terms of both the type of advertising and the target to which it is directed. These include, by way of example:

- national advertising;
- retail or local advertising;
- direct mail advertising (and leaflets inserted in journals);
- advertising to obtain leads for sales staff;
- trade advertising;

▎ sector advertising (for instance, to a particular subdivision of a market such as the SOHO market – the small office/home office part of the market for computers and other office equipment).

A more specific way of understanding what advertising can do is to summarise some of the major purposes of advertising – that is, the various different objectives that can be achieved through using advertising in particular ways. A representative list, which is by no means exhaustive, is as follows:

▎ to inform potential customers of a new offering (from a new product to a product revision);
▎ to increase the frequency of purchase;
▎ to increase the use of a product;
▎ to increase the quantity purchased;
▎ to increase the frequency of replacement;
▎ to lengthen any buying seasons;
▎ to present a promotional programme;
▎ to bring a family of products together;
▎ to turn a disadvantage into an advantage;
▎ to attract a new generation of customers;
▎ to support or influence a retailer, dealer, agent or intermediary;
▎ to reduce substitution by maintaining customer loyalty;
▎ to make known the organisation behind the range of offerings (corporate image advertising);
▎ to stimulate enquiries (from customers or trade);
▎ to give reasons why wholesalers and retailers should stock or promote a product;
▎ to provide 'technical' information about something (this may actually be technical or more general information).

There are clearly many reasons behind the advertising that you see around you (and no reason for some of it – it is just bad; though remember you must try to judge objectively – something may not be designed to appeal to the likes of you). All advertising should be originated with a specific purpose, and doing this – and doing it creatively – is the task of people on this side of marketing. The purposes listed above are not mutually exclusive, of course, and many of those listed apply, or could apply, to one advertising campaign (though trying to do too much at once may risk diluting the effectiveness of any one element of it).

Whatever specific objectives the use of advertising seeks to achieve, the main tasks for it are usually:

- to gain the customer's attention;
- to attract customer interest;
- to create desire for what is offered;
- to prompt the customer to buy (either at once or in the future).

Advertising is, therefore, primarily concerned with attitudes and attitude change; creating favourable attitudes towards a product should be an important part of the advertising effort. Fundamentally, however, advertising also aims to sell, usually with the minimum of delay, although perhaps a longer time period may be needed in the case of informative or corporate (image-building) advertising.

Every advertisement should relate to the product or service, its market and potential market, and as a piece of communication it can perform a variety of tasks. It may:

- *Provide information.* This information can act as a reminder to current users or it can inform non-users of the product's existence.
- *Attempt to persuade.* It can attempt to persuade current users to purchase again, non-users to buy for the first time and new users to change habits or suppliers.
- *Create 'cognitive dissonance'.* This memorable piece of jargon means advertising can help to create uncertainty about the ability of current suppliers to satisfy needs best. In this way, advertising can effectively persuade customers to try an alternative product or brand. (Extreme versions of this are referred to as 'knocking copy' used sometimes by, among others, car manufacturers – which is openly critical of competition.)
- *Create reinforcement.* Advertising can compete with competitors' advertising, which itself aims to create dissonance, to reinforce the idea that current purchases best satisfy the customer's needs. This is maintaining awareness and aiming to continue to prompt ongoing purchases.

Moreover, advertising may also act to reduce the uncertainty felt by customers immediately following an important and valuable purchase, when they are debating whether or not they have made

55

the correct choice. This is perhaps most important with significant products and significant spending (eg a car or refrigerator), but is all part of constant reinforcement.

Types of advertising

There are several basic types of advertising and these can be distinguished as follows:

▋ *Primary*. This aims to stimulate basic demand for a particular product type, for example insurance, books, tea or wool, and includes advertising done by overall trade bodies rather than individual suppliers.

▋ *Selective*. This aims to promote an individual brand name, such as a brand of car, toilet soap or washing powder, which is promoted without particular reference to the manufacturer's identity.

▋ *Product*. This aims to promote a product or range of related brands where some account must be taken of the image and interrelationship of all products in the mix.

▋ *Institutional*. This covers public-relations-type advertising, which in very general terms aims to promote the company name, corporate image and company services; the organisation might advertise overall without mention of the various products or services that comprise its operation.

Advertising communicates through a variety of media and must be created and executed creatively with an appropriate strategy in mind if it is to be successful.

Advertising media

There is a bewildering array of advertising media available. These include daily, Sunday and local newspapers, magazines and colour supplements, television and radio, outdoor advertising (eg posters and litter bins), cinema, exhibitions and a plethora of other media from matchboxes to the side of the space shuttle (once used by Pepsi) and the now-ubiquitous Web site. Any can be considered for any business, though the right mix for any one business will vary, and some methods are simply not right for some products.

For example, not every company can afford television advertising or wants the broad coverage it provides. Some media are simply not cost-effective in certain circumstances; you are unlikely to see, say, an individual small retailer advertising on TV, but may well do in a local newspaper or on a poster in the shopping precinct. Advertising sometimes assumes greater importance because of its other linked characteristics – an advertisement alongside an editorial mention (perhaps generated by public relations) may work much better than one without this editorial link.

All advertisers must make their own decisions (advertising agencies handling the larger advertising budgets have sophisticated media buying departments), not only about different methods, but about exact media – one newspaper versus another and so on. It may even be that a specific page in a publication pulls best, and costs most to use.

Not all advertising, however, is aimed at potential consumers; some is directed at intermediaries.

Trade advertising

This is certainly important, and in many industries advertising is split between that directed to ultimate customers and that directed at those in the channels of distribution. It is often not sufficient to advertise products to consumers alone, particularly where it is important that distributors and retailers are willing to stock and promote a product.

Even though the sales force has a prime role to play in ensuring that stocking and promotion objectives are achieved, trade advertising also has an important role to play in this respect; indeed it sets the scene for such sales visits. So some advertising is visible only in trade circles or, in industrial marketing, in media with a technical bias. Nevertheless this is an important aspect of advertising.

Advertising effort needs to be spread amongst the various target audiences that match a particular product. Trade advertising may take a large share of this on occasion. It must be tailored to the trade, which probably wants to hear different things from the ultimate public and potential customers, and be spoken to in a different way. The basic principles of what makes advertising work and the strategy involved are similar for all types of advertising.

But advertising is more than a series of individual advertisements. It reflects, or should do, an overall game plan – a strategy – which coordinates what is done, producing a cohesive whole directed at achieving the desired results. Advertising needs to be designed and produced in a way that reflects an analysis of the market and a subsequent sensible choice of media and advertising strategies. This means those involved – more than one person is often involved – must be in close communication.

If advertising effectiveness is to be maximised then it must be carefully planned and originated. It may help to spell out what needs to be done in a simple strategy document. At its best, such an advertisement strategy statement is brief and economical, and does its job in three paragraphs describing:

▌ the basic proposition – the promise to the customer and the statement of benefit;
▌ the 'reason why' or support proof justifying the proposition, the main purpose of which is to render the message as convincing as possible;
▌ the 'tone of voice' in which the message should be delivered – the image to be projected, and not infrequently the picture the customer has of him- or herself, which it could be unwise to disturb, or rather, wise to capitalise on.

Even with a clear strategy in place, advertising remains as much an art as a science. The most famous saying about advertising is that of the company chairman who said: 'I know half the money I spend on advertising is wasted, but I do not know which half.' This is a remark that contains a good deal of truth, and a sobering thought with regard to budgets, every penny of which has to be fought for in many organisations.

The next question is how an advertisement can be made creative. There are many ways: humour, personalities, exotic locations, cartoons, even running advertisements in the form of a serial, ending with a cliff-hanger to encourage viewing the next. (Gold Blend coffee was the first to use this, at least in the UK, albeit on TV. The company even ran press advertisements saying no more than the time and date of the next instalment. This campaign was very successful, and provides an example illustrating that new ideas can be found and sales can rise as a result.)

In other words, advertising needs to be creative. Often its task is to make something routine, or even potentially dull, 'interestingly different'. Just occasionally the product really is interestingly different; more often the essential qualities of the product need presenting in whatever way allows the presentation to persuade.

Top tasks

Conference time

You are sales director of a company selling, say, electronic equipment – computers and the like. Technical developments mean that the product range changes regularly as new features are added to existing products, and new and upgraded products are added. Revenue targets are challenging and you are conscious of being in a dynamic competitive industry. In a week's time the company's annual sales conference is scheduled. Sales staff are congregating from all over the country; it is an important event that carries a high cost both in money and in the time it takes up. What transpires at it will set the scene for how the sales team approach their task over the weeks and months that follow – and thus the influence on sales results is direct and specific.

The event must inform, instruct and enthuse. You must finalise and send out the agenda in a day or two. What topics do you list? And how do you handle them in order to maximise the effectiveness of the event and send people away feeling it was useful and fun?

Job implications

Even the brief run-down on advertising that space permits here gives a flavour of the job to be done. Elements of this are highly creative, for example advertising agencies tend to be informal organisations, inhabited by young, seemingly casual people, who in fact work under high pressure and are often regarded as being 'as good as their last idea', something that can range from one slogan to a whole campaign. It also has a scientific side: efforts are made, despite the difficulties, to measure advertising effectiveness, select media scientifically and run a tight ship in terms of the logistics and interface between advertising and the rest of the marketing, indeed corporate, activity. It does little good, for example, to have a major advertising campaign, designed to launch an expensively developed new product, break before the product has been delivered to the shops.

There are plenty of top jobs here, ranging from head of specialist functions in an agency (copy-writing, perhaps) to advertising manager in a company where much of what is done is done through an agency (which is only as good as the briefing it gets).

What is more, similar situations exist in the areas of all the other promotional techniques. In all of these the points made about advertising – the need for organisation, clear objectives and strategy, creativity etc – apply in similar ways. While not going into detail about them, the other methodologies are noted here with brief comments.

Public relations

This is often abbreviated to PR (which also, with the typical confusion of marketing terminology, stands for press relations). Public relations is concerned with the overall image of an organisation. The question here is not whether an organisation will have an image. It will. The question is how to make the image a good and positive one. Public relations people are concerned with everything that shows, particularly the graphic image of the company (everything from business cards to the side of delivery trucks) and press visibility.

Press relations

Though comment on this began above, it deserves its own heading. Positive coverage in the press is an important part of a firm's overall promotion (so too may be the occasional fire-fighting that is necessary when bad publicity occurs). Press relations people are communicators who need to understand the media (press, television and radio). They must liaise with them and also internally (perhaps persuading a reluctant technical person to be a spokesperson on, say, local radio). Specialist skills and approaches are necessary here. Again those who head up this function may see it as a top job in its own right or look beyond.

PR makes a good example of the nature of the many more specialised job roles in marketing. So here again a job description is taken from *The Marketing Workplace*.

PR manager/director

Description

The development and coordination of all policies and programmes relating to all the phases of public relations activity.

Personal specification

▌ graduate-calibre individual with a minimum of 10 years in marketing communications and five at senior level in public relations management gained within a commercial environment;

▌ a thorough understanding of the principles of effective communications internally and externally, mass media, publicity, advertising, education, community relations;

▌ ability to plan and present ideas and concepts effectively to gain support of the business and any appropriate third party;

▌ highly analytical – the individual will need to be able to assess data from numerous data points and recommend tactical steps to execute;

▌ excellent relationship and networking skills, with the management ability to direct project efforts.

Suggested professional qualifications (CIM)

▌ CIM Postgraduate Diploma in Marketing (DipM);
▌ chartered marketer.

Responsibilities

▎ Plan and create implementation road map and schedules for all public relations activity to support brand and communications strategy. This will involve liaising with the leaders of the business and corporate headquarters to ensure that communication is consistent across geographic territories and across all layers of the organisation.

▎ Evaluate all existing programmes, services, techniques and procedures, and establish the annual calendar for installation of programmes.

▎ Work closely with the head of human resources to ensure that policies and programmes are explained to all new employees, and procedures governing talking to the press are covered. Create company guideline document for all existing and new employees to protect legal and confidentiality issues.

▎ Participate in local community and with national bodies to gather information, and seek support of those groups where necessary to ensure the profile and position of the business remains whole and develops.

▎ Play a key role in, or even direct, the internal communication programmes through various methods: e-mail, group meetings, company communications.

▎ Ensure key people and/or products are covered in industry and business press to support brand campaign and enhance sales effort. Manage the PR agency to develop articles and so on within core and vertical media.

▎ Work as part of the senior management team to understand key business messages and interpret to deliver business solutions messages.

▎ Develop budget and gain approval through marketing or business owner of the P & L.

▎ Foster a rapport with the media and create mutually respected relationships.

▎ Contact the media to ensure coverage of innovative programmes, positive developments, employee promotions or acquisitions.

▎ Substantiate and where possible quantify changes through market research.

▌ Be expert at minimising risk and deploy risk mitigation exercises where necessary.

The space available precludes quoting a full job description at this length for every job under the marketing umbrella. However, this example, from a core but specialised area, shows something of the detail involved in such jobs. Every job needs to be specified clearly, so that it can both operate effectively and gel neatly with others throughout the marketing operation in any given organisation. Now, further job areas to consider include:

▌ *Sales promotion.* This term encompasses a mass of techniques including competitions, point-of-sale material (that used in shops), sponsorship and a range of devices such as brochures, leaflets and newsletters as well as promotions hung around a list of 'devices' (such as 'buy two, get one free'). It is another creative part of the communications mix.

▌ *Direct mail.* Often decried as 'junk mail', this is a major medium, and for some organisations their main (or only) form of promotion. For many, direct mail works: it is flexible, easier to test and measure than many other mechanisms of promotion and much harder than it might look to get right. So again there is a specialist breed of marketing people whose expertise in this area puts them in what again are top, albeit specialist, jobs.

▌ *Web sites.* A variety of electronic media is now in use. The simplest are no more than a modern alternative to the brochure. But more sophisticated things are happening here too. Again specialists are called for, and this creates more jobs with a unique – and technology-based – brief under the marketing umbrella. There is a problem though. Some of those attracted to this kind of work by their technical prowess are 'head-in-the-clouds' techno-wizards who would not recognise a customer if they fell over one. Somehow what is done in this area must be given a customer focus – and ensuring this creates more jobs.

Promotion in all its forms is an area where new ideas are always in evidence, indeed must be, and where much of the marketing battle can be won or lost. The result is that there are some key jobs to be done here – it is another area that may suit in its own right as well as being a route to the top.

The sales force and the sales job

There is an old saying that nothing happens until someone sells something, and in many businesses selling is indeed a vital part of the communications mix without which the rest of the promotional activity can be wasted. Selling is the only persuasive technique that involves direct, individual, personal contact.

Now let us be honest: selling can sometimes have an unfortunate image. Think of your own instant judgement on, say, a double-glazing or insurance salesperson. The first words that come to mind may be 'pushy', 'high-pressure' or 'con-man'. Selling can be associated with pushing inappropriate goods on reluctant customers; selling sand to Arabs, perhaps.

All this may not put you in mind of a job you want any part of, though it remains a valid starting-point for some of those going into marketing. The best – that is, most effective – selling can be described as 'helping people to buy'. Much of it has advisory overtones and, if it is to be acceptable as well as effective, it cannot be pushy, but must, like everything in marketing, be customer-orientated.

Selling is, in fact, a skilled job. It demands a professional approach from the field force that carry it out. (*Note* There are other kinds of sales role, for example on the telephone. These tend to be more specialised, sometimes lower-level and perhaps more difficult to move on from.) Customers may want the product but, with plenty of alternative sources of supply, they are demanding, and convincing them to do business with a particular supplier may be no easy task. The right approach is essential.

Perhaps the following apocryphal story (taken less seriously from my book *Everything You Need to Know about Marketing*, published by Kogan Page) makes the difficulty of the task clearer.

Buyers are a tough lot

It is any buyer's job to get the best possible deal for his company. That is what they are paid for; they are not actually on the salesmen's side, and will attempt to get the better of them in every way, especially on discounts.

This is well illustrated by the apocryphal story of the fairground strongman. During his act he took an orange, put it in the crook of his arm and bending his arm squeezed the juice out. He then challenged the audience, offering £10 to anyone able to squeeze out another drop.

After many had tried unsuccessfully, one apparently unlikely candidate came forward. He squeezed and squeezed and finally out came a couple more drops. The strongman was amazed, and, seeking to explain how this was possible, asked as he paid out the £10 what the man did for a living. 'I am a buyer with Ford Motor Company,' he replied.

Buyers are not really like this; they are worse.

However and wherever, selling must take place if the marketing process is to be successfully concluded. At one end of the scale it is simple. For example, an off-licence may be able to increase sales significantly just by ensuring that every time members of staff are asked for spirits, they ask, 'How many mixers do you want?' Many people will respond positively to what has been called the 'gin and tonic' effect, the linking of one product with another. Sometimes the question is even simpler: for example, the waiter in a hotel or bar who asks 'Another drink?' is selling.

At the other end of the scale, sales do not come from the single, isolated success of one interaction with the customer. A chain of events may be involved, several people, a long period of time and, importantly, a cumulative effect. In other words, each stage, perhaps involving some combination of meetings, proposals, presentations and more meetings, must go well or you do not move on to the next. The customer has the right to opt out at any stage.

So with the thought in mind that the detail of what is necessary will vary depending on circumstances, let us review the stages in turn and some of the principles involved throughout the sales process. Selling starts, logically enough, with identifying the right people to whom to sell. Sales time is expensive, so it is important for salespeople to spend time with genuine prospects, the more so when a longer lead time – typical in the purchase of, say, computer systems – is involved. Some of the right people come forward as a result of promotional activity. They phone up, return a card from a mailshot, or whatever and, in so doing, are saying 'Tell me more.' Others have to be found; finding them – prospecting – is the first stage of the selling process in some businesses.

The professional sales approach

It is beyond the scope of this book to describe the whole sales process in detail. (I have done that in *101 Ways to Increase Sales* (Kogan Page) – if a book on marketing cannot contain a few plugs of this sort, what can?) Some details, however, are worth mentioning.

First, the basics – to be successful, field sales staff must be able to:

- *Plan.* They must see the right people, and the right number of people, regularly if necessary.
- *Prepare.* Sales contact needs thinking through. The so-called 'born salesperson' is very rare; the best of the rest do – and benefit from – their homework.
- *Understand the customer.* They use empathy – the ability to put themselves in the 'customer's shoes', to base what they do on real needs, to talk benefits.
- *Project the appropriate manner.* Salespeople are not always welcome. They cannot always position themselves as advisers or whatever makes their approach acceptable; being accepted needs to be worked at.
- *Run a good meeting.* They should stay in control, direct the contact and yet make customers think they are getting what they want.
- *Listen.* This is a much undervalued skill in selling.
- *Handle objections.* The pros and cons need debating; selling is not about winning arguments or scoring points.
- *Be persistent.* They need to be able to ask for a commitment, and if necessary ask again.
- *Manage accounts.* This is so as to hold existing business and develop ongoing business across the range for the future.

Such people are managers of their time, territory and customers; it is a role that demands a good deal of self-sufficiency and dedication as well as persuasive communication skills.

Secondly, a variety of additional skills may be necessary to operate professionally in a sales role. These include:

▌ account analysis and planning;
▌ the writing skills necessary to ensure proposal/quotation documents are as persuasive as face-to-face contact;
▌ skills of formal presentation;
▌ numeracy and negotiation skills;
▌ computer skills (increasingly so).

And all this in a job whose holders are sometimes described as being 'only in sales'. It may not be where you want to be for ever, but a spell there can provide valuable experience for anyone aspiring to get to the top in marketing.

Selling is sometimes regarded as other than an important part of marketing (something this section has been at pains to contradict). If it is so regarded, that is a big mistake, and any organisation taking this view may well suffer for it. Sales really is the final link with the customer, and if it is not working well tricks are being lost. Selling is as much a strategic element of marketing as any other.

Sales management

Closely linked to the topic of the sales process and the sales team who are involved in it is the role of sales management. It is not enough for a company to simply push salespeople out into the market and say, 'Sell.' Much as anyone else, salespeople need managing, and managing in a way that maximises their performance. This creates what is perhaps the top staff-management role under the marketing umbrella, that of sales manager (or director, as such a position is often at board level). Usually such a manager is very much part of the overall management and marketing team. In a large company, with many people on the sales team, there may be several people at different levels: area managers, sales manager and sales director. In a small company, the 'sales manager', whatever he or she is called, may have many tasks and responsibilities that are really general management functions.

In addition, the person managing the sales team will usually handle a certain number of customers, usually larger ones, personally. There is nothing wrong with this; indeed such involvement is useful, but it can dilute the time available for the classic sales management functions and this, in turn, can leave sales less effective than might otherwise be the case. Certainly it would be my observation that in industries that put suitable time into managing a sales team the investment it represents is regarded as both necessary and worth while.

What exactly does a sales manager do? Most usually, the classic tasks of sales management are regarded as falling into six areas, which reflect the need to:

▌ *Plan*. Time needs to be spent planning the scope and extent of the sales operation, its budget and what it will aim to achieve. Achievement is organised first around targets, and setting targets, not just for the amount to be sold but for profitability, product mix etc, is a key task. If the product range is large then this makes it especially important that the team's activities are directed with the right focus.

▌ *Organise*. How many salespeople are required needs calculating (not just a matter of what can be afforded, but of customer service and coverage, though the two go together), as does how and where they are deployed. This must also address the question of the various market sectors involved, looking at not just who calls on customers in, say, Hertfordshire, but how major accounts are dealt with and the strategy for any non-traditional outlets, which may well need separate consideration. Organisations that sell to groups of customers differing radically from one another may separate the different sales tasks, and even have separate sales teams.

▌ *Staff*. This is vital; it is no good, as they say, 'paying peanuts and employing monkeys'. If the sales resource is going to be effective then it must be recognised that recruitment and selection need a professional approach, and the best possible team must be appointed. The job is to represent the firm, to differentiate from competition and sell effectively – certainly and continuously. Recruitment may be a chore, but selecting the best of a poor bunch (rather than re-advertising and starting the whole thing over again) should simply not be an option. It is evident from even a cursory scan of typical job advertisements how much emphasis is put on past experience in many industries. As people tend to be sought at a youngish age (when they are cheaper?), maybe more fresh blood might be usefully contemplated by some. The experience route is fine, but one effect can be to encourage the duds to circulate around a particular industry, and if someone only did an average job for one company, what makes it likely that he or she will suddenly do better for another?

Train. Perhaps develop is a better word here, as the process is ongoing. Because there is no one 'right' way to sell, what is necessary is to deploy the appropriate approach day by day, meeting by meeting, customer by customer, and continue to fine-tune both the approaches and the skills that generate them over the long term. If the team is to be professional in this sense, then more than a brief induction is necessary; an ongoing continuum of field development is necessary. It is simply not possible to run a truly effective team without spending sufficient time with individuals in the field, using accompanied calls first to observe and evaluate, and then to counsel and fine-tune performance. Without this, performance can never be maximised; indeed a whole area of activity is going by default. Although results show what is being achieved, figures alone cannot, by definition, show how things are being done in the field and whether performance could benefit from fine-tuning. Only by direct involvement can sales management put themselves in a position to know what action might improve performance, and take it. Many would regard this as certainly the single most important aspect of the sales management job. The reason is entirely practical – time spent on it acts to increase sales. Not least, the process is valuable in ensuring that salespeople adopt a practical and constructive approach to what they can do day to day to refine their own techniques and improve performance. Whatever the support given by sales management, the salespeople themselves are, after all, the only coaches who are there all the time.

Motivate. Like development, motivation does not just happen (this is true of so much in management). It needs time, effort and consideration. Salespeople spend a great deal of time on their own – and are exposed to the attrition of the attitude that can come from customers who are not exactly 'on their side' –

and as a group need considerable motivation. Like training, motivation is not simply a 'good thing'; it increases sales and makes performance more certain. Again sales management must work at this area systematically. It affects overall issues such as pay and other rewards (for example, any commission scheme must act as a real incentive – not simply reward past performance – and thus must be well conceived and arranged). Motivation also affects many smaller issues. Just saying 'Well done' is an element of motivation; how many managers, whatever their role, can put a hand on their heart and swear they have found time to do even that sufficiently often in, say, the last month? There is so much involved here – communications, effective sales meetings and good organisation; for example, letting a salesperson act without good support material to show may well make selling more difficult and thus be demotivational. This is especially so if struggling salespeople feel that only inefficiency somewhere in the organisation has caused their difficulties. So motivation has a broad remit and involves a wider group of people than the sales manager alone.

Control. Constant monitoring is necessary if the team is to remain on track and thus hit targets. Action must be taken to anticipate and correct any shortfall and this is traditionally the role of control. It is at least as important, however, to monitor positive variances. If something is going better than plan, then it needs to be asked why – maybe there are lessons to be learnt from the answer that can help repeat the good performance or spread the effect more widely.

All in all, sales management has a wide and vital brief. The quality of sales management can often be readily discerned from the state of the sales team. Excellence in sales management makes a real difference. Time spent on all aspects of sales management can have direct influence on sales results. Again this may be an area, and a natural progression from sales, that is worth further investigation. Time spent in this position can be very rewarding (and if you want to manage people this is somewhere you may want to stay as a top job in its own right). Alternatively it can provide a solid stepping-stone leading in the right direction.

Brand management

Brand or product management jobs have long been important posts. Part of the organisation of many firms promoting a number of different products (especially in FMCG companies), people in these jobs were described earlier as mini-marketing managers. As such they may have complete responsibility for the marketing of that brand (a sales force selling several brands may be an exception to this).

To understand what the job entails, we need to consider a little about branding. Any product needs a name. Simplistically this can be something like Bloggs Biscuits, and if Mr Bloggs owns the company that makes the biscuits this may be the only reason for adopting the name. More often in marketing the intention is to create a product characterised and made memorable by its name, so that the combination of name, product and product characteristics – including subjective factors such as image – are part of what motivates people to buy.

Sometimes this is achieved with a simple name: Smiths Crisps continue to do well despite a very simple approach to their name. Sometimes agencies are employed, midnight oil is burnt and a name is only decided upon after long deliberation. There are all sorts of considerations: is it catchy and easy to pronounce, does it look good in print and does it work internationally (and not have some unfortunate meaning in Italian)? But there are no rules. Who would have thought a name like I Can't Believe It's Not Butter (for a butter-like spread) would work? It is surely far too long, but it does work, at least for the moment, and has inspired other extra-long names conceived on a copycat basis.

Companies work at this process, and names may change and evolve over time: BMW surely sounds better than the Bavarian Motor Works. Such reduction is not uncommon: British Telecom reducing its name to BT, for example. There are many different approaches to name, and there is more to a brand than just a name.

Branding encapsulates the whole concept of creating a product and giving it an appealing image (one often targeted on a specific group of customers – a market segment). It gives rise to other

71

jargon phrases used to define various subsidiary processes that are involved:

▌ *Brand image.* This is the image that goes with the total product or brand creation, for example the identification of Audi cars with excellence of engineering, and thus performance, safety and more. It is the detail of this definition and analysis that links to exactly how the marketing of the brand takes place and evolves over time.

▌ *Brand positioning.* This refers to the position in a 'scale' of similar, competitive brands and which position is selected for a particular brand – how high or low the price should be set, how popular or exclusive the brand should be, how practical or fashionable etc.

▌ *Brand personality.* This is a slant on brand image, one that emphasises the character of the product rather than the more tangible aspects of it.

▌ *Brand extension.* This is a term referring to a particular use of branding. Brands tend to be equated with particular products. If successful, they create a powerful force for sales, building loyalty and making repeat sales more successful. Brand extension takes this franchise in the market and uses it to create products in different areas that gain from the image created where the brand name was originated. Some examples make the concept clear:

  – Mars bars and Mars ice-cream (different, but not so different a product area);
  – Porsche cars and Porsche watches (very different);
  – Virgin airline and cola and bridal shops (again very different).

You can probably think of other examples. There is a strategic choice here. Not all companies operate this way, and too much brand extension can become confusing for the customer and thus self-defeating.

▌ *Brand values.* This refers to the need to keep a brand's personality within bounds, in other words not to overextend the image trying to make it all things to all people. To take an extreme example, it would be overextending brand values for Rolls-Royce to promote their high-quality cars as the best vehicle to nip to the shops in.

Branding may tend to be applied most often to FMCG products, but the concept applies equally in other areas, and is relevant and referred to in industrial and business-to-business products, for example computer brands (which perhaps combine aspects of both consumer and industrial products), and even something like jet engines for an airliner.

Top tasks

A new... what?

You market a successful product with a long history and a well-established brand name. Further sales growth is now more difficult as market share is already high. Growth is perhaps better pursued by adding to the product range and engaging in brand extension – using the brand name for other products (in the way Mars did so successfully in adding ice-cream to their confectionery range). The failure of any new product would not only be a disaster in its own right, but it might well adversely affect sales of the original product and would certainly risk diluting its image.

Whatever new product is chosen to extend the brand in this way must be selected with care. How do you come up with suggestions and how do you decide what should go forward and become the first new product to extend the name?

Job implications

The product manager has to create the brand and instigate a programme of marketing activity to promote and sell it success fully. This really does encapsulate the whole marketing process. Product managers:

▌ produce marketing plans;
▌ oversee or conduct research;
▌ develop products (and set up test markets and new product launches);
▌ plan promotional campaigns;
▌ monitor progress;
▌ constantly seek ways of creating an edge in the market.

They must also liaise with colleagues internally, for instance ensuring production and distribution are supporting their efforts to gain their share of the time and concentration of the sales force. Customer contact may be important too. Certainly with FMCG products, where major customers hold such power, this is vital.

A senior brand manager post is often a top job in its own right, and can lead on naturally to marketing management and marketing director positions.

The distributive chain

Finally in this chapter, a word about the opportunities inherent in the distribution process, which is part of the marketing cycle. What exactly does distribution mean and why is it necessary? Marketing must link to the market, not just in terms of having a focus on customers and their needs, but literally. Goods and services have to be got to market, and direct contact created with buyers. Distribution is what allows this to happen.

Let us take general principles first. However good any product or service, however well promoted and however much customers – and potential customers – want it, it must be got into a position to give them easy access to it; it must be distributed. And this can be a complex business, though it is certainly a marketing variable, albeit one that many regard as rather more fixed than it in fact is. Consider the variety of ways in which goods are made available. Consumer products are sold in shops – retailers – which may vary enormously in nature, from supermarkets and department stores to specialist retailers, general stores and more – even market traders. These may, in turn, be variously located: in a town or city centre, in an out-of-town shopping area, in a multi-storey shopping centre, or on a neighbourhood corner site.

But the complexity does not stop there. Retailers may be supplied by a network of wholesalers or distributors, or they may be simply not involved; some consumer products are sold by mail order, or door to door, or through home parties (like Tupperware). A similar situation applies to services, even traditional banking services being made available in stores, from machines in the street and through post and telephone – even on a drive-in basis.

Banking is also an example of the changes going on in the area of distribution, many of these developments being comparatively recent moves away from solely traditional branch operations. Business-to-business industrial products are similarly complex in the range of distributive options they use. The revolution of e-commerce adds even more possibilities.

Areas where change has occurred, or is occurring, can prompt rapid customer reaction if whatever new means are offered are found to be convenient. Old habits may die hard, but if change is made attractive and visible then new practices can be established, and these can then quickly become the norm. Conversely, if the distribution method is inconvenient for customers then they will seek other ways of access to the product (or simply not buy it), though sometimes inconveniences are tolerated because need is high or compensated for by other factors. For example, there are some who will put up with queues in one shop only because the alternative is too far away, or has nowhere convenient to park.

How a company analyses the distributive possibilities and organises to utilise a chosen method or methods effectively is certainly important to overall marketing success. Analysis can be assisted by a process called market mapping. This looks graphically at the range of options and the different routes available or in oper-ation; it is useful to analyse what action is necessary to create the flow desired along each channel. The example market map shown in Figure 4.1 illustrates the concept and shows the position for the publishing industry. Where you bought this book (maybe from a bookshop, an e-tailer or whatever) will be there somewhere.

Job implications

There are two points to be noted here. The first concerns the distribution task, a further key task that marketing must accom-plish. Choice must be made about distribution – which method or methods to use. Then the channel selected must be made to work. The communication with those intermediaries making up the points along the chain is crucial. Sales may be influenced directly by how well the likes of distributors or agents are managed and motivated. The challenge of getting all this right is made more difficult if distribution must be achieved on an international front.

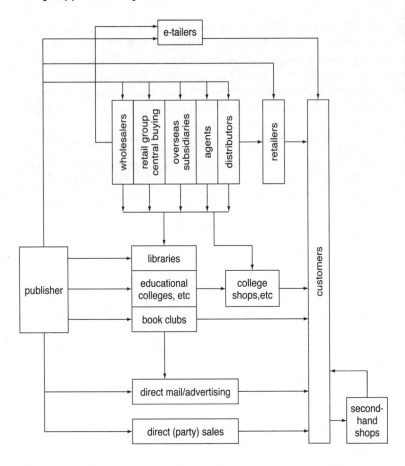

Figure 4.1 Market map showing distributive chains in publishing

The second point to note concerns the jobs within distribution. The distribution pattern inherent in the marketing of goods and services extends the choice for those seeking a career in marketing. The manufacturer (or originator) of a product (or service) is not the only option; marketing jobs exist throughout the network. For example:

▊ Retailers, especially those with multiple branches, need marketing (a shop manager could be the first step to being marketing manager of a retail chain).

▌ Distributors (agents etc) are often big businesses in their own right and whoever heads them up needs to inject marketing expertise too.

▌ A constant searching after new ways of providing distribution (some of them linked these days to e-commerce) provides further opportunity for those adept at this sort of innovation.

Distribution is a major part of the marketing scene. Top jobs certainly exist here. Daisy Hyams, who used to be CEO of Tesco, was once called the most powerful woman in Britain. It was a description with which many of her suppliers readily agreed. Many of the organisations and people who make up this scene are certainly influential; what they do makes a real difference.

This much should be sufficient to give an overview of the work undertaken throughout the marketing scene. Remember that in all these areas particular jobs can vary. For example, the job of managing a field sales team is different from that of managing a team in a telephone call centre. In any area there will be top jobs; however, we now move on to examine what might be called the ultimate top job, that of marketing director.

5 Heading up the marketing function

In this chapter we examine the nature of the top marketing job and the characteristics necessary for those who undertake it. As was said early on, in any organisation someone must 'wear the marketing hat'. The task of marketing cannot be effectively undertaken piecemeal. It needs someone who oversees, coordinates and manages the activity and does so from a position of authority within the organisation. This most often means that such a person is at board level.

It might seem also that, given the scope of marketing, it is a broad brief. It is. It is fine to be the head honcho, but it is in the nature of top jobs that they are not a doddle. More seriously they would not be so satisfying – and would not command significant rewards – if they were something just anyone could do.

So, whoever the marketing director is (it might even effectively be the general manager in a smaller firm), what does he or she need by way of characteristics? Several areas are important and all have relevance in thinking about careers.

Competence in marketing

The first point to be made here relates to the principal marketing techniques and methodologies. There are eight major tactical areas of marketing: market research, product development, pricing, distribution (an area that these days might need to include aspects of e-commerce), the full plethora of promotional techniques (public relations, advertising, sales promotion) and selling. While it is unlikely that any one individual will have similar experience and expertise in all of these, it is important that some experience exists across the board, certainly if sensible decisions are to be made about the marketing mix.

So the marketing director needs to be something of a marketing jack of all trades. In any particular industry, however, there may be techniques that are especially important (as the organisation of promotional events often is in a professional services firm, or sponsorship in industries linked to the world of sport). In this case the marketing director must match such priorities with his or her own experience.

In addition, there are few industries where the marketing director is not involved personally in some element of customer contact (if only with major customer relationships), so the necessary personal and persuasive communications skills are always going to be a key issue.

Management skills

Another common requirement is for people management skills. The senior person normally has staff (in a large company a whole marketing department), so must be able to recruit and select appropriate staff, develop and motivate them and plan, organise and control the activities in which they are involved. Similarly, working with people around the organisation and outside the organisation, for example those in an advertising agency or other specialist supplier, may be involved and important also. Project management skills are also necessary.

It is largely through these first two, and linked, factors (competence in marketing and management skills) that the all-important coordination of marketing activity is executed. It is also worth noting that effectiveness of coordination is one factor that acts to differentiate competing organisations.

Directorial ability and perspective

There is a real difference between being a manager and being a director. First, the legal basis of the director's responsibilities should be noted (though this is outside our brief here). Beyond that, the marketing director must be able to do the following:

- Understand the other related functions across the organisation in order to fulfil his or her role as one member of the top management team.
- Take a corporate view, balancing considerations in the light of the best course for the organisation as a whole rather than for

one particular department. This can be a delicate business. The functional responsibility is clear, and the focus there is on marketing. Yet as a member of the top management team, there is a separate and equal responsibility to act from that perspective and not to take an exclusively parochial view.

▍ Take a long-term view, certainly longer that that often appropriate in management (where a good deal hangs around the financial year; in some industries, as has been pointed out, time-scales are longer than in others).

▍ Set long-term objectives and create strategies designed to achieve them.

▍ Influence the implementation of marketing, incorporating the policies and priorities involved, and ensuring that the management team (and supporting staff) are able to see those policies and priorities through and make them work.

All this implies that the marketing director has a range of skills that underpin the job to be done – for the ability to succeed is important also (the relevant skills are investigated in Chapter 8).

A 'marketing' style

No one management style is 'right', of course, in marketing or in any other function, for that matter. Indeed it would be a great pity if the personality of individuals brought nothing to bear on the way they did their job, or if all that was necessary was a slavish following of some 'best' approach. On the other hand, the most effective approach to marketing seems, from experience, to be broadly 'scientific'. That is to say it is systematic. Identification comes first – of problems and opportunities, say, to keep it general. Data is collected and analysed, solutions and possible approaches are sought, a prime option is selected, and tested if possible, implementation follows and the results are monitored and used to influence future decisions. It is an approach that is at once open-minded – objective – and which is not seduced by fashion, apparent universal solutions or personal prejudice – 'It was my idea, so it must be right.'

Being open-minded must also be related to change. Change is inherent in the world of marketing. Markets, products, methods, customer demands and expectations – perhaps especially the latter – all are subject to rapid change. The marketing director must be comfortable with this, adept at changing and moving fast in response to change – better still, adept at anticipating change and keeping the organisation ahead of the game. Remember, it is a creative role too.

The cynical view of planning is that it consists of anticipating the inevitable and then taking the credit for it. In fact the marketing director must be adept at planning winning strategies. There are no guarantees (remember the art and science description of marketing). What seems like a good idea at the time can be stillborn or fail in a very visible way. One example that comes to mind is the change made in image recently in British Airways. This involved the incorporation of various artistic designs into the overall graphic image of the company, of which the most obvious element was the livery of the planes – each tail fin carried a different ethnic design. The plan cost a sum involving tens of millions of pounds, yet very quickly, after a period during which the only reaction was fiercely negative and mounting criticism, a similar sum was spent to change again. One cannot imagine that so public a failure did the career prospects of those senior people in the organisation who may have championed the change very much good. Indeed the CEO has since been changed.

The point remains – to stay at the top in marketing you need a good track record. Some mistakes may be inevitable (after all, making none at all might be evidence of too conservative a policy and style), but success – which is easily measured in marketing – is a mark of those who move ahead.

Top tasks
Friend or foe?

As marketing director you have plans to develop a range of marketing activity to fuel the growth the company seeks. Such plans need funding and this demands that the company as a whole makes choices. As a director you have a dual responsibility: first, to the functional area you represent; secondly as a board member – alongside others – with a responsibility for all aspects of the organisation's well-being. On occasion this produces clashes. For instance, one director wants to invest in new equipment to keep up with the IT revolution; another wants research and development funding increased to secure the long-term future; another sees the priority as moving to larger premises.

You have plans to combat predicted competitive activity. Available finance is finite: compromise is necessary. The next board meeting must set priorities and make decisions. What line do you take?

Accelerated experience

Being marketing director is not a job many, if any, people could do as their first assignment; still less is it a job you are likely to be appointed to with no experience (well, not unless you form your own company!). That said, what experience do you need to have, beyond what has been addressed as characteristics, to be able to sit in the hot seat?

There are several factors to bear in mind here:

▌ *Qualifications.* The need for qualifications is dealt with elsewhere, but quite apart from what having a qualification will do for your profile (and your CV), obtaining a qualification is itself helpful. You gain in two ways: 1) in terms of the knowledge gleaned during the course (and there is a lot to know about marketing); and 2) in terms of the process. Early on in life (perhaps before gaining real business experience) a course for a significant qualification will expose you to doing a variety of things at a stage where they are new to you. These include things such as decision making, problem solving and other matters that will need to be second nature later in your career.

Such courses can involve other elements too. One that is worth mentioning is the involvement with the world of business that a course may involve. 'Work experience' is a generic term to cover it, but it can provide much more than the brief term suggests. It may even be that a course involving this kind of experience is chosen intentionally, precisely because it is so valuable. It can plunge you into situations that provide a very real contrast with the academic world in which the rest of a course may be taken. Recently I was with a client in Prague, and one of the people I met turned out to be on such a secondment. He was working in a different country, a unique market environment, with a large multinational organisation. The local office was small, however, and an extra pair of hands was rapidly being involved in a wide range of matters across the board within the operation, many that would normally be in more senior hands – a very special learning experience.

Training. Learning is a continuous process, certainly in marketing. Given the dynamic nature of so much that is encountered in working in marketing, a constant process of updating is necessary. This is not the same for many skills. Consider a simple example. If you learn (formally or informally) keyboard skills then, provided they are used, you will be able to type at some speed. If practice continues, your skills will be maintained; it will be possible actually to say, 'I can do this', and no more learning may be necessary (unless technology changes keyboards radically). This is simply not the case with most marketing skills. You are only ever able to write a marketing plan, interpret a research report, or sell to a major customer in a way that works now. What needs to be done in future on these and many other matters will be different, perhaps radically different. You spend a lifetime refining such skills. Much of this comes through experience (experience of which you take note!). But some of it comes from continued training. For many people, of course, all this is a good thing – it is precisely the constant change and challenge that appeals to them about marketing.

So, during your career everything from attending courses (even for a day or two) to reading a book will contribute to what you can do in future. It is worth noting that the Institute of Marketing now has – as part of its recent chartered status (it is now the Chartered Institute of Marketing) – a CPD (Continuing Professional Development) scheme. This is something that has existed for many years in other professions such as accountancy. It recognises the need for continuing training, and awards chartered status to individuals who register and keep up with a prescribed programme of development activity (more of this in Chapter 8).

▌ *Career experience*. It should also be clear that past career experience influences the ability to do well in future. The trick is to get experience fast, specifically the kind of experience that will fit you for the top job. On the one hand there is a risk in moving jobs too often (and too rapid a series of changes may not appeal to those who judge your CV as you apply for new jobs). On the other hand you will benefit from having assignments that extend the range of things you can do, indeed from choosing carefully what you do and perhaps what you do not do. If you have specific career intentions, then you need to identify the skills this will demand and try to organise to obtain appropriate experience along the way.

▌ *Updating*. Beyond the formal matters mentioned in the sections above, many people find that a number of other involvements, formal and informal, are useful to extend and accelerate their experience. For example you might do the following:

- Join and attend (or serve on the committee of) professional bodies such as the Chartered Institute of Marketing, the Marketing Society (which has more of an emphasis on FMCG marketing), or similar organisations with an industry or functional focus (eg the Professional Services Marketing Group and the PM Forum in professional services, or the Market Research Society in market research). There is a thriving regional network of branches in most bodies of this sort.
- Make a point of networking to create and maintain contact with people who can further your experience and career (remember networking is a two-way street – you only get out in line with what you put in).
- Attend relevant conferences (for both the content and the people you will meet); indeed, you may present at such events.
- Acquire a mentor. Regular guidance through the valuable, but informal, relationship between someone and a person (usually, but not always, more senior) prepared to take an interest and assist is a real asset. It may be well worth while

to seek out a mentor, or mentors; certainly my own career would have been radically different, I suspect, without a particular person I have been lucky enough to have in this role over many years.

Anything along these lines may play a part; it is an area that is worth some thought and some action.

Top tasks

Persuasive processes

You are at the final stage of a long sequence of events leading up to making a major sale. The prospect telephoned and spoke to someone who sent further details. This was successfully followed up, a meeting was set, written proposals were put in, surveys were conducted, samples were provided and further meetings were held. Months have passed. Each stage had to be well handled or the prospect would not have gone forward to the next. So far, so good. You are now short-listed and will be one of three potential suppliers to make a formal presentation to the prospect's board. Nothing is decided yet; there is everything to play for and a great deal hanging on what happens next. There will be no second prizes; you either get the project – or not.

You have your sales hat on. You have to organise the team, decide what is to be said, by whom and in what order. You have to coordinate the team's efforts, make sure their visual aids look good together and that you take no more than your allotted time. You ask yourself the final question: above all, how do you tackle it in such a way that you stand out – positively – and differentiate yourselves from your competitors?

They say that the higher up the tree you go the greater the danger of falling off. Marketing is certainly an exposed occupation, and an element of risk goes with the territory. But risk is reduced by competence. Everything mentioned here, however, plays a part. If your career has a good start, and if your experience grows certainly, specifically and substantially – and at a good rate – this helps. So too does the attitude and action you take.

You need to see the development of your career, your progress towards a top job, as something you must actively work at. The actions you take as a result of adopting this attitude must be considered and appropriate. Everything matters. Attention to detail is important. One extra contact, the decision to join a particular committee, attend a certain conference or take a particular course, or even just to read one book, may assist. In the end it is the cumulative effect of all your career development action, in the context of the events of your actual career, that takes you forward.

Getting to the top can involve a lucky break. More likely it involves a series of smaller incidents of good fortune, being in the right place at the right time or whatever. Realistically the lesson to draw here is that any good fortune that may come your way needs you to spot it and take advantage of it.

But never assume this will happen. Good luck is not to be relied on. It may never happen. But you are always there, and the action you take – literally day by day – through your career can make a difference; indeed you do best to assume that it is the only thing that will.

We will end this chapter by again taking a job specification from *The Marketing Workplace*, CIM's guide to job descriptions, this time for a director-level marketing job.

Board director – client-side

Description

Operating at strategic and tactical level you will manage, lead and motivate your department or division in addition to contributing fully at board level.

Personal specification

▌ successful track record at senior manager/director level in managing and developing a marketing business or function;

- experience in operating successfully at strategic executive level and tactical implementation;
- manifest commitment to achieving results and the ability to persuade and influence at senior levels;
- demonstrable track record of leading, motivating and developing individuals;
- proactive style and drive, coupled with a real commitment to team work;
- excellent leadership and communications skills;
- strong commercial and business acumen;
- excellent negotiation, presentation and relationship-building skills.

Suggested professional qualifications (CIM)

- CIM Postgraduate Diploma in Marketing (DipM);
- chartered marketer.

Responsibilities

- contribute to overall strategy, performance and profitability of the company;
- take full profit and loss responsibility for department/ division, ensuring that profit forecasts are consistently achieved or exceeded;
- establish business plan, operational goals and objectives;
- oversee the running of the activities of the department on a daily basis and, as such, be accountable to the managing director for its performance;
- ensure that all activities are delivered to agreed time/cost/ service specifications;
- continually identify quality and service improvements and ensure these are integrated into future activities;
- be fully responsible for all personnel within the department, overseeing career development, training and motivation;
- ensure that existing customers and potential new customers genuinely receive a quality-focused service;
- anticipate and develop strategies to meet internal and external business needs;

▌ regularly interact with executive-level management, working with colleagues to promote the best interests of the company.

Now we move on. The next two chapters examine particular areas that may be important to the top job that you want: jobs with an international dimension and jobs with an involvement with e-commerce.

6 *International opportunities*

One of the four 'P's that are factors making up the classic marketing mix is place. A business may be successful on a limited geographical scale, for instance operating only in one major city. At the other end of the scale there are multinational businesses that span the globe. Witness the posters you see on landing at almost any airport in the world: names such as Coca-Cola, McDonald's, Hewlett-Packard, Compaq and many more appear everywhere.

Marketing that involves overseas markets – on whatever scale – can be interesting, a challenge and add a whole separate dimension to the marketing job. There are further choices to be made here in terms of the elements you may want to see in your marketing career. Essentially there are three overriding issues to consider from a personal point of view:

▌ *Scale of operations.* If you want to work for a large organisation, there are many that are international in some way. Conversely, picking an international firm usually puts you in the league of those organisations that are large. Products and services play a part here: soft drinks are needed across the globe, but some other products are more specialised and do not offer export opportunities. Such scale also relates to risk, and this is worth a thought. A large company may be stable, but it is possible to be quite a big fish in one geographic pond with a multinational, and yet wake up one morning and find that a US parent company has made some change that leaves you nowhere.

▌ *Travel.* A personal goal may be to travel. Fine; certainly being involved with a large international operation of some sort may allow you to do just that. Travel can be something that occurs unexpectedly. In my own career, while travel was not something

I sought or thought likely, company growth took international form in part. So now I find business has taken me to most countries in Continental Europe (including certain of the old Eastern bloc countries), to the Far East, Australia and New Zealand, parts of Africa and both North and South America; and to some of these on a regular basis. Most of this travel I have enjoyed; certainly once it was under way I worked at ensuring some of it continued. But make no mistake: travel can get out of hand. Living out of a suitcase, endless flights, time changes and time in hotels can quickly pall, and too much time away from home can disrupt home life and career alike. This is another area about which you may want to form a considered view as you plan your future.

▌ *Overseas residence.* To experience overseas working and not get the disadvantages of too much travel, some people prefer the resident route. Actually living in another country – becoming an ex-pat, as it is called – guarantees a different sort of experience, though it is possible to lose touch with home base (so much so that you may come to be regarded as inappropriately qualified to work there again). Certainly this route is only for those able to adapt and fit in with the culture and way of working in another country.

The world is now, we are told, a 'global village'. Certainly, for many organisations success must be measured amongst world markets. The foreign currency generated by international operations is vital to the national economy, so there is also an additional worthwhile element to work that involves this. I am, on occasion, what is called an 'invisible export' (providing services) and add to these figures just a little.

An international element to your career may be something that comes, or is sought and found, early on or which develops over time. It certainly extends the definition of 'top job'. A few people may become overall marketing director for a major multinational, but many more may head up operations in a specific region or individual market.

Top tasks
Where next?

You operate a chain of speciality retail shops selling a tightly defined range of products in a niche market. Expansion has progressed well. You have outlets in most major cities and in other specialist locations such as airport shopping areas. Growth must continue. The physical geography restricts 'more of the same'; there are simply not many uncovered areas of the country left to exploit. Other options must be considered: overseas development, shops within shops, a sub-brand of outlets selling different products, or maybe different ways of selling existing products. Each presents a different challenge; some need different expertise or resources from existing operations; and the risks vary too.

Ideas abound, but you are at the stage where specific plans must be championed and one course of action pursued. How do you proceed?

To consider career options in more detail, you need to review the strategies used by organisations to explore and exploit overseas markets. Several approaches are involved:

▌ *Export marketing.* This is essentially selling goods to overseas customers but doing so from a base in your home market. Essentially it implies physically shipping goods across the world. This may be done by the organisation itself, for example using its own fleet of trucks to ship goods to Europe or beyond. It may be dependent on the use of shippers, whether goods are to travel by road, rail, air or sea. It can be done with no support or presence in the final market; but it may necessitate some presence. (*Note* This is an area that demands specialist knowledge of such things as export documentation, shipping, insurance, credit control etc, as well as marketing.)

▌ *Export with a local presence.* The form that a local presence takes clearly affects the way a company operates and thus the nature of the jobs involved. Maybe the company will have:

- – Its own local office. This will link with the headquarters and may handle independently a range of things that have to be done locally (and maybe differently from the way they are done at home) – local advertising or service arrangements, for instance.
- – An agent or distributor. This is a local company that undertakes the local work and marketing on behalf of the principal. Such a company may specialise, selling only, say, construction machinery. Or it may sell a wide range of products, sometimes across the whole range of industrial and consumer products in the way large distributors – often called trading houses – do. Sometimes such arrangements are exclusive, meaning the agent will not sell products for competing manufacturers; sometimes the arrangements are not exclusive. Payment is often on a results basis, but the agent cannot simply be set up and left to get on with it. Success is often in direct proportion to the amount of liaison, support and communications instigated between the two parties by the principal. An active approach is necessary. For example, the distributor's sales staff must understand the product and know how to sell it. A company may well see this as an area for support: they provide training, flying trainers out to the territory and taking any other action necessary to make it work (translation of materials, perhaps). Another kind of top job would be to head up marketing in a trading house.

- *International marketing*. This implies a greater involvement in the overseas territories, everything from setting up subsidiaries to joint ventures and, in some businesses, local manufacture. The complexities here can become considerable, with components being sourced from several different locations around the world, assembled in one or more main centres and then distributed to and sold in many markets. This is common in the motor market, for instance.

- *Licensing*. This is an example of one of the other approaches possible. Here nothing is done on an ongoing basis by the principal, which sells the right – the licence – to produce the product to someone else. The deal may include help with a variety of set-up processes (from the provision of drawings to machinery), but thereafter the local company runs its own show and marketing, and payment is on some sort of 'per product produced' basis.

▌ _E-commerce_. A more recent development is the phenomenon of business that may, in a sense, operate anywhere in the world from anywhere in the world. This is another area of growing opportunity for marketing people.

Top tasks
Enhancing performance

You sell an industrial product of some complexity. Customers need extensive advice prior to purchase and the product needs maintenance thereafter. Overseas you sell through distributors. Many of these are large organisations in their own right and sell a range of products. Your product must compete, therefore, with others for the time of the marketing and sales resources of the distributors, and for their people's time, attention and expertise. You have detected a weakness in the sales ability of many of the distributors' sales staff. This you believe is reducing their sales effectiveness on your behalf. They need good product knowledge, but they also need better interpersonal and persuasive skills. The obvious answer is to train them.

You need to ensure that the distributors, which you can only advise, do this. How can this be done? Can training be offered from HQ? Who would undertake it? How do you make it attractive to the distributor management? Should they pay for it? And, most important, how can you make it have a real impact on the sales of your product?

There are other methods also: for instance _franchising_, well known from the likes of McDonald's, but used with a wide range of products and services. Marketing's job is to select and use methods appropriately, and maybe to originate new ones.

Throughout industry, some companies sell what they produce in similar form world-wide. Others tailor the product to individual markets – even something as simple as a chocolate bar may have many different recipes and flavours for each of many different markets. This applies to many aspects of a product: cars may need change to meet local safety standards, books need translating, electrical products may have to work with different voltages etc. It can simply be arrogant to assume no change is needed, so marketing logically demands consideration of such options and that adaptations are made as necessary.

The marketing principle of 'knowing your customer' is clearly paramount in overseas markets where people, culture, customs and more may be very different. Such differences will potentially affect not only details relating to the product – for example, a number may be popular in one country and regarded as unlucky in another (as 8 is regarded as auspicious by the Chinese) – but also the manner of doing business. Here such things as the prevailing practice regarding negotiation, business ethics or time-scale may all be different. Even a name – of a company or product – may need careful checking; what sounds catchy in English may be lewd in German or hilarious in Urdu. (It is unlikely that certain overseas products – Sweat, a Japanese drink, or Nora Knackers, a Norwegian crispbread – will ever do well in the UK.) Another key factor of marketing overseas is the increased commitment necessary; people, resources, money are all spread more widely.

If success is to be had, it needs an appropriate commitment in these terms, to ensure a chance of success. It also demands that operational factors respect different geographic conditions. Some markets – France, say – are small for certain traditional British products (like jam). Others – for example, the South-east Asia region – are largely English-speaking, so will buy more English-language books and magazines than, say, Taiwan. Distance is important too. Singapore may be 5,000–6,000 miles away from the UK, but customers there are in some respects no different from those in the UK or anywhere else: they want to be looked after. There is no substitute for personal contact. If you want to operate overseas, you must go overseas. Not only can more be done face to face, but physical presence in many territories is read as commitment. All this affects the people involved and the jobs that it is necessary to organise.

Again this is an area that illustrates the dynamic nature of marketing. The world itself is changing as we watch: new markets are opening up and, at the same time, some markets may contract (for reasons as varied as government change to natural disaster).

It is also an area where those who are responsible for marketing may not have the same level of support as may be available at home. The UK marketing manager may inhabit a large office, surrounded by staff and support services. The equivalent position in another country may be one of a handful of people. Posting a letter may mean going to the post-box personally. Briefing a major customer may mean a visit 'up country' in a four-wheel drive vehicle on roads made treacherous by the rainy season.

In addition, always remember that there are jobs here that involve a whole additional dimension as compared with home-based marketing posts: that of getting to grips with a different culture. It may be subtly or radically different. Extremes may involve marketing people politely eating sheep's eyes in the Middle East or trying to remember the etiquette involved in a meeting to negotiate terms taking place in Japan. Beyond difference, you might also like to consider hostility. Some countries are not an automatic choice for comfort. A range of things – climate, politics, law and order or lack of it, or simply inaccessibility – may make them unattractive as places either to visit or to live. For some this is something to avoid; for others making a specialisation of being able to operate despite such difficulties creates a career opportunity.

However you look at things, it remains in most ways a big world we live in. Geography is certainly a potential decision area for many people thinking about how to develop their careers.

7 Marketing and e-commerce

Let us be clear right at the start – this chapter is out of date. The pace of change means that by the time it has got into print, and you read it, things will have moved on. Having said that, it should not matter, at least not within a reasonable time-frame, as what is most important here are the trends, and the attitudes to information technology (IT) that must be taken with regard to marketing. If you are computer-literate, more so if you have real expertise in this kind of area, then marketing is a prime place to consider taking your talents. But how exactly is marketing being affected by the ongoing IT revolution?

Some general points first. The pace of change is frantic. Even considering the longer-term, things move fast. Computers have revolutionised the office environment, but not everything has progressed as predicted. Consider the following:

▌ Computers themselves have perhaps evolved faster than initial predictions, but what for instance has happened to the 'paperless office'? Most people's desks seem as submerged as ever (and some of it is computer print-out).

▌ Computers make things more efficient and do things faster, but how long does it take to get to grips with the latest feature and why have such phrases as 'Sorry, it's in the computer' become the ultimate excuse for delay?

▌ Computers have reduced costs, but what about the cost of the equipment, and of the training and the peripherals they make necessary?

These considerations, and no doubt others, expose two sides of the proverbial coin. There is truth in both aspects of them. It is too simplistic to expect just to be able to say, 'Computers make things better' and expect there to be no downsides. The point about change remains. It took some years for computers to become

established in every office, proportionately less for them to prolif-
erate on to every desk so that now most executives take it as read
that they will type a good deal, perhaps all, of their written output.
It took even less time from the introduction of e-mail to the point
where you were not seen as a serious player without it. Indeed,
'instant communications' have become part of the culture of many
organisations since. Further new things may well consume us all
even more quickly. We will see.

At the same time the pace of change does make problems. The
cost of re-equipping or updating machinery, the training – formal
or informal, it all takes time – and so one seem to continue in an
endless cycle; and those are just examples. A new development
may be real and useful, but to many people it sometimes seems to
last about five minutes. The little ditty below summarises the
feelings of many people as they are faced with the next new gismo:

> I bought a new computer
> It came completely loaded
> It was guaranteed for 90 days
> But in 30 was outmoded.

Though maybe such sentiments are only possible because of the
computer industry's marketing success.

Top tasks
The right person

You have helped your company respond to the Internet revo
lution. You advocated the company having a Web site in the
early days, set clear objectives and created a basis for the site
that was successfully set up – it worked well and has been
updated and expanded. Now, initial success indicates that a
whole new area of e-commerce is ripe for development. You
have put up plans for this, obtained agreement and a budget
that includes a new appointment: someone expert in elements
of e-commerce to head up the development programme and
take the plan forward to grow the business.

Now you have to find such a person. You need to create a job description and a profile of the person needed, recruit (through some appropriate method) and interview candidates. Some help is on hand from the company's human resources department, but it is a crucial task – finding the right person can make the difference between the new development being a success or a failure. How do you ensure you pick the right person?

The impact on the world of marketing

So far, examples may seem to be primarily in the area of office administration, but the electronic revolution has wide impact. In marketing, three areas deserve particular mention – products, methodology and electronic marketing.

Products

The evidence for electronically influenced products is all around us. This includes things that are obviously electronic such as the current profusion of computers, computer games, digital cameras and personal organisers. It also includes things that appear to be just 'electric' such as washing machines and fax machines, and others such as cars – but how many chips are there in all of these, and more? More products in the future will be in these general categories. Maybe some of them will be things you will market. The whole process of product development in these circumstances becomes very different to the development of simpler things. Original development may:

- take longer;
- cost more;
- be more complex (and thus more likely to be problematical);
- be more vulnerable to competition.

We can all think of examples of the latter. Facsimile machines saw off telex in a moment. E-mail is replacing many fax messages (less special fax paper sold, and more normal paper as messages are printed out), cassettes were largely sent on their way by compact discs, and a variety of music and video formats currently vie with one another to be the next 'standard'. This kind of dance is typical of many fields from software to toys; only the time-scale varies. Updating may follow very quickly. In some product areas new versions follow one another almost on a monthly basis. If such a scene appeals, and you have the characteristics to fit into this world, then maybe here is the beginning of an answer to the question posed earlier about 'marketing what?'

Methodology

The way things work is being changed by technology. Right across the business world, the range of change is enormous. Think of the role that electronic money transfer and 'hole-in-the-wall' cash machines (coupled with postal and telephone accounts) have had on bank branches; think too of the developing impact of Internet banking and where that may take us. Such things constitute big changes, and quoting such an example barely scratches the surface of what is going on.

Things change everywhere. Customers used to go into a shop, select goods, pay their money and that was the end of it. Paying now involves electronic machines at the cash points. These do not just facilitate the taking of money (and make it possible to employ staff who cannot add up!); they are the tip of an electronic iceberg of integrated computer systems. The cash point registers the sale, communicates with stock control and more supplies of a product can then be ordered automatically when stocks decline to a certain level. If a customer uses a card (increasingly so-called 'smart' cards), whether a credit card or one linked to a loyalty scheme, the sale can be recorded against an individual. Buy product X and the customer suddenly starts receiving promotions through the post for product X or its competitors (something like a supermarket can charge its suppliers to send this sort of material on its behalf). Such schemes can be linked back to the cash point, so that offer coupons are distributed to particular customers in a way that reflects their buying record – or rather, of course, in a way intended to influence their future buying practice.

Again space prohibits a lengthy list of examples but the current complexity and future possibilities are clear. For any particular organisation there are matters here that must be coped with. For example, a supermarket might be more resistant to seeing salespeople if its computer system is able to reorder directly and automatically. Such salespeople (or their marketing masters) then have to find new ways of prompting the discussions they want, discussions that go a long way beyond reordering and involve promotion, display and much else, and which are vital to the marketing effort.

As well as difficulties there are also opportunities, areas where an organisation can choose to get involved, despite greater complexity, if it sees an advantage. For example, a search of what is new and an assessment of how it might help have become a prerequisite part of marketing thinking. Examples may well date, but the following show what is now possible, what you might get involved in working on and indeed what is now normal in terms of ways of going about things:

▌ Computers can now calculate optimum merchandising arrangements. A company making a range of products different in size, price, margin and rate of turnover can work out what mix of product selection should be put on any particular amount of shelving that a store allocates to its brand at the touch of a button. No spare space is then left on the shelf, and turnover and profit generation are maximised.

▌ Field sales staff now routinely carry computers and can use them, for instance, to give an instant answer to customer questions about stock and delivery of a product.

▌ Customer details can be accessed instantly during transactions just by the mention of, say, a postcode; this facilitates many processes, for example dealing at a distance from a call centre.

▌ Mobile communications (in all their growing forms) allow orders to be placed from anywhere and at any time.

▌ Computer models can allow experimentation with such variables as price, allowing the effects of proposed changes to be anticipated in advance.

▌ Profitability of individual major customers can be calculated and trends predicted.

Computer and other IT developments will doubtless produce many more advances of this sort, all either actively assisting marketing effort, or with which marketing must fit in if it is to retain credibility.

Electronic marketing

The other major area, and one subject to continuing change and development, is the whole area of the Internet and e-commerce. This tends to be spoken of as if it was something new. In fact, though how it operates is clearly new, the effect it has is to add to the choice of methodology available in two different areas: promotion and distribution. Thus saying you want to go into an e-business is no different to saying you want to work for a retailer; you still have to decide on the nature of the firm and on what will be sold – similarly with services. Let us take promotion and distribution in turn:

▌ *Promotion.* Web sites, for all their technical wizardry, are only another method of communicating with customers (and some-times – see distribution below – of doing business). Consider Web sites, first and foremost, as a promotional channel. As such they must command attention, put over their message clearly and act to persuade. They must also be convenient and easy to use. At this stage, and for a while yet, this means appealing to people who see themselves as other than at the forefront of computer literacy as well as e-enthusiasts. A Web site may be an electronic alternative to many things: a brochure, a salesperson, a showroom or shop window, a magazine or more (in any combination). Setting it up, making it desirable in the way it works and integrating it with the rest of an organisation's marketing activity is quite a task.

▌ *Distribution.* Here we are in the territory of what has become known as e-commerce. This is a situation where the whole business transaction, or most of it, takes place over the airwaves, as one might say. The point about clarity and conven-ience made above is perhaps even more important here. Some things are up and running and working well. Customers may conduct their banking and finances through Internet accounts; they may order many things – computers, pizzas, books, CDs etc – from Internet sites. One point about this that will be worth watching is the relationship between Internet shopping and conventional retailing. There is much change in train here.

Top tasks

Brought to book

You are in charge of marketing for a book publisher. The industry is changing rapidly. Major retailers are bringing pressure on margins, e-retailers – like Amazon – are changing the way people buy books, and every other day the newspapers are telling the public that books are about to be replaced by some sort of electronic gismo that can put the equivalent of an encyclopaedia in their pockets. One possible avenue to increase sales is to find new methods of distribution. One publisher, for example, sells children's books at Tupperware-style coffee mornings hosted by mothers of preschool children.

Can you think of something equally different that can increase your trade without antagonising the retailers on whom you are currently dependent?

Some things can work fine exclusively through Internet channels. If people want to buy a new novel by a favourite author, they are probably happy not even to look at it – they tap into Amazon.com or whatever, call up the title and place their order (with maybe a little price comparison along the way). Other purchases are more complex. If people want a new CD player, say, they may well want to look at it – better still hear it and check it out. They go to a retailer and do just that. Then they might elect to visit a number of sites on the Internet, compare prices, check delivery and so on, and place an order with one. What many people will not do is simply order a machine seen only on a computer monitor screen.

In other words retailing is currently necessary for certain kinds of e-commerce to work. How this pans out and what future buying practice will be like is still uncertain. That said, e-commerce works well for many things, the fields in which it operates are growing and more and more people are either experimenting with this sort of shopping or, having tried it, are expressing confidence in it and becoming regular users. Current predictions for the further future include the demise of supermarkets as we now know them. All bulk and heavy goods, from tissues to cat food, will be ordered over the Internet and delivered. Customers will only visit stores for things that demand real choice or checking; as a result stores will be smaller, but departments such as the bakery or cheese counter will expand. Again we will see.

Even this amount of commentary is more than sufficient to show the possibilities, and to show also that whatever may be happening now is just scratching the surface. Marketing is likely to be at the forefront of all such change; again the opportunities are clear.

Job implications

Two points need to be made here. First, it is clear that considerable elements of this kind of technology have become an inherent part of many marketing operations. In effect, the normal methods of marketing of many products and services demand some knowledge of this area. Much of the detailed work (of something like setting up a Web site) is probably not going to be carried out by the marketing person, but the job does involve specifying what must be done and getting this aspect of the marketing process working in the right way.

Secondly, this is an area for innovation. Some marketing people will have to initiate new activities in these kinds of area (relating to both products and methodology). And there is certainly a minimum level of talent necessary for this sort of thing – you cannot, after all, recognise the possibilities if you have no feeling for this area at all. Further, there is an increasing number of businesses for which the IT possibilities are fundamental – as for an e-tailer such as booksellers Amazon. There is no clear picture here yet; some such companies are now well known, successful (in the sense of having many satisfied customers) but, as yet, unprofitable. Others have been and gone in a moment, or once started rapidly became part of something else. There will be those –

currently in existence or yet to arrive on the scene – that are destined to become major players.

The businesses that operate within technological areas, or which market technologically based or influenced products, will all need marketing people who are up to a considerable, and very particular, challenge. Maybe your future lies in something futuristic.

8 *Key attributes – skills and qualifications*

All sorts of abilities are difficult to acquire. It takes time and effort to learn to do many things – juggle with flaming torches without burning holes in the carpet, perhaps. But marketing is something of an oddball in this respect. First it demands a range of skills – in marketing and in management – and these in turn demand both study and experience to acquire. Secondly, the mix of necessary skills varies depending on the area of work – a range, as we have seen, running from research to copy-writing and beyond. Further, someone may have a whole package of skills, qualifications and experience and may still be precluded from certain jobs because one element – essential to that job – is missing; or because he or she does not have the elements of business acumen and creativity marketing demands.

No one has 20/20 foresight, but it is worth thinking through as far as possible what skills your own long-term desired future demands that you acquire. Clearly certain specialised areas may make special demands; for instance, there are marketing jobs that need:

▌ fluency in a foreign language (see Chapter 6);
▌ technical qualifications (eg in engineering or accountancy);
▌ high levels of one particular skill (eg writing good, creative and persuasive copy for someone working in an advertising agency);
▌ skills linked to a specific industry or area of work (eg numeracy in financial services);
▌ a certain level of formal qualification in order to have credibility in a certain field.

Beyond that we can focus on certain common skills, and some – referred to as career skills because they are so often instrumental in assisting career development when they are present – that are always likely to be helpful. Many of the latter are simply prerequisites of success; they are not options.

The right skills in the right form

Skills are required in specific form. For example, if their use is crucial to marketing outcomes, then they must be deployed not just skilfully but in the precise way that the nature of the operation demands. For example, a salesperson may not just have to conduct a customer meeting, but have to do so in a very short time (eg medical representatives calling on doctors are often fitted in amongst appointments with patients and are granted an average audience of four minutes). A marketing manager may need to make not just a good presentation (eg at an overseas dealer convention) but one that is spot-on 20 minutes in duration to fit with the event timetable, despite being simultaneously translated into Spanish. A press officer may need not just to give an interview to the media, but to be bright-eyed and bushy-tailed at 6 am after a long journey to a regional radio station in time for a live appearance on its breakfast show.

In other words, skills are no use if they can only be deployed in 'perfect' circumstances; they have to be made to fit and work in the real-world situations of the organisation and its market environment. Whatever is being done and whatever skills need to be deployed in doing it, other factors can usefully enhance it: native wit, flexibility, a pragmatic approach, an ability to be 'quick on your feet' and more besides.

Skills are referred to throughout the book, and readers should be under no misapprehension regarding the range involved and their inherent importance. In part, marketing is a matter of flair, but much of it involves solid, considered, effective and systematic application of the skills and approaches needed in both marketing and management.

Top tasks
May I help you?

In a service organisation, people, and how they interrelate with customers, are vitally important. In recent years your company has streamlined its customer contact; a series of sales offices have been replaced by two dedicated call centres with customers encouraged to make contact this way. It works too; a significant proportion of orders placed come in over the telephone. But service is vital. Success increases the volume of contact and resources are not keeping up with demand. Waiting time has increased; so too have the number of customers complaining of waiting too long, of soulless automated telephone systems and staff who, seemingly under pressure, are less polite and efficient than they might be.

Unless the operation is brought up to scratch, and fast, sales will suffer. How do you improve performance? Where do you start?

Qualifications

Qualifications are of dual importance to anyone with an eye on career success. They are: 1) a method of acquiring knowledge and developing skills; and 2) evidence of a level of competence in a particular area.

With a high proportion of people entering business having some sort of qualification, it is important for marketing careerists to consider carefully what they need to do. Again some of the issues have been mentioned and there are choices to be made. You need to consider first whether you want to work to secure a qualification. If you do:

▌ At what stage of your career do you do so?
▌ In what way do you undertake it? (Methods range from a full university degree course to a correspondence course or distance learning, perhaps utilising the Internet.)

▌ What area do you select – an overall management degree or diploma, perhaps with marketing focus, or something functionally based, for instance in advertising or market research?

There are both broad and specific ways of approaching these questions, and the range of options is very wide. For example, if you decide to do a degree course, marketing will be represented in many universities and in specialist centres such as business schools. A careful and thorough trawl through these circles must be undertaken, and the relative merits of the various options assessed. It can be a daunting task. What is more, it has various dimensions. You need to decide which course will be the best, and most relevant, learning experience. You must consider which will be judged most attractive by potential employers (if you know at this stage what kind of people and organisations these are likely to be). You must consider too a host of other factors such as the social element of the experience and the location in which it will take place.

What qualification?

This is an area for careful consideration (and therefore some advice is useful). There is no easy option here. I cannot say, 'Take this degree course and your marketing career is set for success.' There is a host of options and people go into marketing and succeed with everything from an HND in some specialised topic (design, say) to an MBA in marketing from a world-renowned institution.

It is beyond the scope of this book to review every option, much less to try to place them in rank order or match the best option to particular career paths. Whatever stage you are at, if you know – or have a good idea – what you want to do, then you can relate decisions to that goal. This applies literally from subject choices in school onwards; and, of course, bear in mind that early exam qualifications may open or close options at higher levels to you if they are required entrance requirements.

Although it is not the only provider of marketing qualifications, the Chartered Institute of Marketing should be a prime point of reference for many people. It offers:

▌ a range of specific marketing qualifications at the various levels;
▌ links with a wide variety of educational institutions that teach for Institute qualifications;

▌ the possibility of using different learning mechanisms (for example, it has recently linked with the Open University to make available a new master's degree in marketing);

▌ dynamic updates to its programme (for example, the e-Marketing Award, to link with the important developments in IT and e-commerce).

The summary of the Institute's offerings shown in Figure 8.1 provides an overview of the different programmes and levels and the relationship between them. A parallel range of qualifications is offered through the Institute's sister organisation, The Institute of Professional Sales, and many of the bodies representing specialised areas of marketing (and listed at the back of the book) also offer qualifications in their chosen field, for instance the Market Research Society.

A successful career in marketing is made more likely if you accept the premise of this chapter: that it is skilful work and – for all that flair can add – success is dependent on the purposeful acquisition of the knowledge, skills and qualifications that make a professional approach possible.

Summary

Good, sound and appropriate qualifications, skills and experience are the foundation of a successful career. One final point is worth mentioning here. Marketing is apt to be an especially fast-moving theatre of activity; indeed this may well be one of its attractions. But this can mean people are caught out. An opportunity materialises. Perhaps a project is looking for someone to take it on, but there is a specific requirement that the person chosen has a particular skill or category of experience. There is no time for someone without it to fill the gap, and such a person may be passed over. Ditto promotion. So early decisions are important. Gradually, as experience builds, qualifications may matter less in relation to that experience; but what is learnt through achieving the qualifications stays with you throughout your career.

Figure 8.1 Chartered Institute of Marketing qualification programmes

Of course, the ability to take on new things and learn fast 'on the run' is itself a characteristic worth having, and this alone may get some people into new areas. But one cannot rely on this. In some circumstances good luck, muddling through and winging it are not options (though they may explain the success of your rivals!); success comes to those with the ability to create it.

The moral is clear. Do not postpone action to fill out your range of skills, certainly those that you see a clear need for in the future. In a busy life it is easy to leave things on one side, sometimes until the moment has passed. One minute you are saying that you have a good couple of years to get up to speed on something; the next you need the skill desperately right now and its lack puts your plans at risk. You cannot anticipate everything, but you do not want to look back and have to say that if you had acted differently then you could have used the advantage then gained to help you move ahead. At any point in your career, and with regard to any element that contributes to it, the saddest position to be in is one for which the description starts, 'If only…'

The strengthening of your portfolio of skills is a continuous process (see below how the Chartered Institute of Marketing regard and organise for it); it is one about which it is worth developing some good habits and practices to keep you ahead and on path for the top. Remember too that if you are currently early in your career, then some of the things you may have to be able to do in the future may not even exist now.

Now, where are the matches? I must give those flaming torches another go.

Continuing Professional Development

The Chartered Institute of Marketing takes the need to keep, update and extend skills as a given. Further it believes that the process of so doing should be a formal one, and bestows the status 'chartered marketer' on those who register and satisfactorily undertake appropriate activities to ensure this development. It describes the Continuing Professional Development (CPD) process as 'the systematic maintenance, improvement and broadening of knowledge and skills necessary for the execution of professional, managerial and technical duties throughout a Member's career' and lists the benefits thus, saying that you:

▌ enhance your CV and improve your career development;
▌ keep up to date with change as it happens;
▌ join an elite group of professionals;
▌ improve your competence, your job satisfaction and your prospects.

The process is described thus:

Complete at least 35 hours of Continuing Professional Development (CPD) each year for two consecutive years. Thereafter to keep your position you have to maintain 35 hours CPD each year. You should also be a full Member of CIM (either a MCIM or FCIM), and in full-time employment. If you were elected to membership after 1 October 1998, you must also hold the CIM Postgraduate Diploma in Marketing.

Your Record Card contains details of the criteria which can be used to contribute to your 35 hours of CPD. Document your progress systematically on your Card – and don't forget to collect the required supporting evidence if you intend to apply for Chartered Marketer status. If you are working towards becoming a Chartered Marketer you will need to complete the Record Card to the correct timetable.

Details of the system are available from the Institute. Here it may just be worth adding a note of the 10 categories of activity that are recognised and which help clock up the relevant number of hours (note that the relative contribution of each varies, and that clearly activity within a category needs to relate to marketing). The categories are:

▌ post-qualification studies;
▌ short courses;
▌ distance learning;
▌ language training;
▌ in-company management development;
▌ imparting knowledge;

- conferences and exhibitions;
- committee work;
- private study;
- meetings.

Each of these is defined in some detail; for example, imparting knowledge includes writing books, articles and conference papers, and part-time teaching (so if you had written this book you could add some hours to your record card!).

Even the amount of detail given here shows the seriousness with which the whole process is taken. This is only right given the nature of marketing, and – however it may be done – no one should go into marketing believing that no form of update and extension of experience and skills is necessary once he or she is established.

9 The route to the top

This chapter has only one overall message. That is that career success does not just arrive; it is actively sought and its achievement is the result of what you do. The changing world of work and the need for active career development were touched on in the Introduction, and the reasons for that need, which flow from the whole work environment, will not be repeated here.

There is no magic formula here, no one thing you can do that will put your career on the fast track. There are, however, a number of approaches that you should adopt – and adopt consistently – that together produce what can be called an active approach. The first thing is to have a clear idea of what you want to achieve.

In a world that is increasingly dynamic in almost every respect, what do you need to note about the world of work that you aim to make the stage upon which you will earn your living?

The world of work

Business pundits and economists predict a range of varying scenarios for the future of the work environment. But there is one thing all are certain about – it will be uncertain. We live in dynamic times. The old world of job security, jobs for life, prescribed ladders of promotion and gradually increasing success and rewards has gone – replaced by talk of downsizing (and right-sizing makes it sound no better), redundancy, short-term contracts, tele-working and portfolio careers.

As you contemplate your own career, waiting for things to 'get back to normal' is simply not one of the options. The future of careers for those who do sit back is bleak, and the environment looks set to remain challenging. The US journal *Forbes* had an apt quotation in it recently: 'If you are not bloodying your nose in today's warp speed economy, we have a word for you. Dead.' No one can guarantee a successful career for him or herself, and being in marketing certainly offers no exception to this rule, but it is something that everyone can influence to some degree. Indeed it is something that you surely want to influence. We all spend a great deal of time at work. It is important to make sure that those hours are as enjoyable and rewarding as possible. There is a line, quoted at the opening of this book, from one of John Lennon's songs, which runs: 'Life is what happens while you are making other plans.' It encapsulates a painful thought. There is perhaps no worse situation to get into than one where we look back with regret.

So, with no rigid, preordained career ladder to follow, careers need planning. The question is how to do it. The bad news is that there is no magic formula. Sorry, but you cannot just snap your fingers, shout 'Promotion!' and be made chief executive overnight (or if you can, please let me know how!). You can, however, make a difference if you work at it. The starting-point, especially vital at the start of a career, is knowing what you want, and this needs some systematic self-analysis.

Setting a course

There are several stages of thinking that are useful. First, you need to assess your skills. You may be surprised how many you have in, for example:

- communications;
- influencing;
- managing (people or projects);
- problem solving;
- creativity;
- social skills;
- numeracy;
- special skills (everything from languages to computer usage).

Next, you need to assess your work values. Here you should consider factors such as:

▎ a strong need to achieve;
▎ a need for a high salary;
▎ high job satisfaction requirements;
▎ a liking for doing something 'worth while';
▎ a desire to be creative.

This could be a long list; you might add other factors from travel to being independent or working as part of a team.

You also need to do the following:

▎ *Assess your personal characteristics.* Are you a risk taker, an innovator, or someone who can work under pressure? Consider what kind of person you are and how these characteristics affect your work situation.
▎ *Assess your non-work characteristics.* This includes such factors as family commitments, where you want to live and how much time you are happy to spend away from home.
▎ *Match your analysis to the market demands.* In other words, consider how well your overall capabilities and characteristics fit the market opportunities, an analysis that should include how your qualifications relate to your target area. This will stop you from seeking out a route that is doomed before it starts. If anything to do with computers, say, throws you, then you will have to either learn or avoid areas of work dependent on a high degree of computer literacy (few areas of marketing would allow you to avoid computers – some demand a high level of computer skill).

With all this in mind you can set clear objectives; the old adage that if you do not know where you are going then any road will do is nowhere more true. Aim high. You can always trade down, but you may be more successful than you think and it is a pity to miss something not because it is unachievable, but only because you do not try for it.

From here on the management of your career progress (including your self-marketing if you will) is in the details, and the first step is to realise just that.

Top tasks
Testing, testing...

Plans are in place for a new product launch. Research and development have done their bit and the product is almost ready to join the range and go on sale. The investment has been considerable, and the cost of failure would be large. A final stage of test is called for to ensure everything is as it should be – a test market. Arrangements are in hand for distribution to commence in the area of one regional television network (which will carry the launch advertising). A date is set, and then with a month to go a competitor launches a similar product, also on test (and luckily in a different region).

It looks as if they will complete their test and move to national distribution first. What action do you take? Do you proceed as planned? Do you advance your timing? Or do you skip the test launch and move straight to national distribution?

Perception is reality

Of course, progress is dependent, probably to a major degree, on performance. Whatever job you do, unless you deliver as it were, then you will have little chance of being judged able to cope with more, and promotion may – rightly – elude you. Certainly the role of marketing makes this especially true of it. But other things have an effect too.

Consider an example. Someone is asked to manage a project. It is important. There is a great deal hanging on it and it is multi-faceted. It might be, for example, the setting up of a new way of operating to maximise overseas market opportunities. The person asked may have all the necessary characteristics to do this successfully, be able to do the necessary groundwork, and be thorough and forget nothing. He or she balances all the various – probably conflicting – criteria, and documents a sound recommendation and plan. So far, so good. Then the person is asked to present the recommendation to the board.

Now making a formal presentation is not everyone's stock in trade. The person is nervous, does not know how to prepare, put it over well, or stick to the time given, and it proves, to say the least, somewhat lacklustre. What happens? Do people say, 'Never mind. It was a sound plan'? They are much more likely to take the view that the ideas themselves are suspect; perhaps they act accordingly, putting the whole idea on hold or taking some other action. And what happens next time such a project needs allocating? The person concerned is not even in the running. The likely career effect is obvious enough.

This makes an important point. Many skills are rightly regarded as career skills. In other words, they are not simply important in their own right; they are important to how people are seen and how they get on. Every field of work will have some such factors that are likely to be particularly important, as in fact presentation skills often are in marketing.

Active career management

There is a long list of skills that should be regarded in this way. In many management jobs they include all aspects of managing people, presentation and business writing, numeracy, often these days computer skills, and more general skills such as good time management. Many are to do with aspects of communication. Take time management as an example. Productivity is as important as results. A characteristic of modern organisational life is that everyone seems to have more and more to do. Some people cope with this better than others. They are better organised. They recognise Pareto's Law: the 80/20 rule that a comparatively small amount of activity will give rise to a large proportion of the desired outputs. Not only is life a little less hectic or pressured for the copers, but they are able to achieve more; and it shows. Thus one area of active career management consists, as we have seen, of recognising what career skills can help you and making sure that you excel in them.

In addition, there is a host of other factors that have an influence on how you progress. Who you know is often quoted as being as important as what you know. Some people seem very well connected. But even this usually does not just happen. They probably work at it: they note their contacts; they seek out new ones; they keep in touch and recognise that this is a two-way process. And it helps.

The way ahead

We have seen that active careerists should resolve to be of no other kind, and that they do not rely solely on good luck. They do however take advantage of any good fortune that comes their way. And their planning and positive attitude to the process make it more likely that they can do so.

What is necessary is an all-embracing approach to what is essentially a lifelong campaign. Those who leave no stone unturned, who look at every detail of their work life in terms of the career implications of it, tend to do best. If they have thought through what they want to do and if they have clear objectives, then – while they may not achieve everything they want – they will get closer to their ideal. This is true whether you seek to make progress within one large organisation, or whether you realistically see your career changing several times as the years go by.

For the most part, careers do not happen; they are made. Marketing is no commercial backwater. It deals with competition in the market-place and is itself a competitive arena for those who work in it. You can do worse than start with a philosophy of active career development at the earliest phase of your career, and see your career as likely to be made primarily – by you.

What constitutes career success

Career success can be measured in various ways, certainly of course in terms of rewards. Money may not be everything, but it is important. And marketing can be well paid. Job satisfaction is important too. I am prejudiced, of course, but I cannot imagine a more exciting and rewarding area of business than marketing in which to work. Further, as we have seen, there is a considerable range of different jobs to be done under the marketing banner.

Mentioning this variety again provides a further opportunity to comment on the concept of a 'top job'. Ultimately, top can be taken as meaning just what it says. Perhaps the marketing director – and it is inherently a director-level role – inhabits the top job. But senior positions exist in spades. The product manager in a large company might have more responsibility than the general manager of a small firm – and earn more too. All the component areas of marketing, from market research to advertising to sales, have their own version of the top job. If you define top job too rigorously, you find there are very few of them in any field. Here we take a broader view; indeed the whole nature of marketing suggests doing just that.

Marketing is an area in which success can genuinely mean being 'at the top'. It can provide a combination of satisfaction and reward that is hard to match. Having said that, you still need to know how to get in, and how to get on in it. In the current context a number of things are important.

Achieving results

Year by year success, in most jobs, is assessed through results. In marketing there is no difficulty in measuring these; they are inherent in the results of the organisation, spelt out in sales, profit, market share and growth. A marketing person who consistently fails to achieve these kinds of targets will not find great favour, and in many organisations this can be restated as 'will not last long'.

The first prerequisite of getting to the top is to be successful at what you do on the way. In other words, success at the job is a factor leading to success in career terms. That said, there are other factors that contribute, so always in your career you need to consider what these are. Key ones are reviewed here.

Developing skills

Marketing may be as much art as science, but it is not all informal and creative. Real skills are involved, as we saw in the last chapter and elsewhere. You need to be aware of what you must be able to do and what you must excel at, and look ahead, taking a view of the job you do now and where you want to go in future.

Specifically:

▌ _Define the skills you need._ This is an ongoing process; skills are needed as a routine now that were not even thought about 10 years ago.

▌ _Take action to acquire them._ Whatever it takes must be done: get yourself on a course, read a book, ask a mentor, or watch others. Methods can be formal, such as requesting and attending a course, or informal, such as making good contact with the training department and getting to sit in on their preview of a training film. In other words, progress can be made up of both major and minor steps forward – all may be significant, and it is ultimately the cumulative effect that matters.

▌ _Practise._ Having acquired the basic knowledge about something, you have to use it. Practice really does make perfect; certainly it can improve skills. A case in point, which makes a good example because most marketing jobs demand it, is the skill of making formal presentations. You need to know the tricks of the trade, as it were. At some stage of your career you may need to find presentations to make. Volunteer for things, use internal meetings as an opportunity to present, or get yourself on committees – whatever in your work circles makes it necessary to present regularly.

▌ _Keep up skills._ Finally, do not allow any skills acquired to atrophy.

You can usefully link this process to your recorded achievements and CV.

Acquiring experience

Everyone wants a career that progresses and enhances their experience. Time alone does not automatically do this. You may be expanding experience too slowly, or – at worst – simply repeating it. An active approach here is necessary also. For example, beyond your day-to-day responsibilities a variety of projects can provide additional experience. Some bosses take this view, involving their staff progressively in more and more. See what you need to know, watch for opportunities and discuss this principle with your boss.

It is almost a prerequisite of getting on to work for a manager who fosters your learning. Staying in a position where this does not happen, or at least shows no sign of happening, is something to consider very carefully. There must be some very strong reasons to make it worth while for any real period of time.

Creating the right perception of yourself

Marketing is largely about perceptions. It creates an image that makes people want to buy products and services. Similarly, how people are perceived is as important as what they do – more so in marketing than in many other spheres of organisational life. In whatever sort of organisation you work, one thing is certain – appearances count. Never mind 'Don't judge a book by its cover'; people do just that. How people perceive you inevitably colours their image of you. Your image also signals something about not just what sort of person you are, but also where you sit in the office hierarchy (official and unofficial). It signals to some people whether you are to be regarded as friend or foe, and what power you are perceived as having to promote or protect yourself. Your image affects how people treat you – whether in terms of putting people off trying to get one over on you, or encouraging their assistance for your cause.

So, it's better to heed Oscar Wilde's comment, 'It is only shallow people who do not judge by appearances', and take note of the potential effect of how people see you. After all, we all have a stereotyped image of extremes such as the absent-minded boffin, the computer geek, or the office Romeo, and sometimes also an image of, for example, the grey accountant or the flamboyant advertising person, so you should certainly consider exactly how others see you. The moral is to use the fact that judgements are made (snap decisions too) and act accordingly. The result here is that you should:

▌ accept the importance of appearance;
▌ be conscious of both the positive and negative sides;
▌ actively respond to the ways people see others, striving to create and put over the right profile.

The starting-point to action here involves some self-analysis. If you know how you want people to see you, then it may be easier actively to seek to achieve the effect you want. This may seem easy. You may want to look powerful, persuasive or professional. But many such fine-sounding words are in fact just umbrella terms – you must ask what being professional, say, really involves. If you made a list it might include such characteristics as being:

- expert;
- well organised;
- well prepared;
- confident;
- knowledgeable;
- experienced;
- trustworthy;
- honest;
- approachable;
- a good listener;
- decisive;
- capable;
- powerful;
- diplomatic;
- skilled at communication;
- loyal.

The above is by no means a definitive list, though many of the qualities listed are certainly important for most people. You can probably add more, including some factors that are more specific to your own current job. Maybe you need to come over as financially aware, as a good negotiator or as a whiz with information technology. Maybe it is important that you are professional in a more parochial sense: seen to be powerful because you have the ear of someone specific on the board, say.

In any case, several points are clear. First, however you look at it, such a list contains a number of factors: perhaps a considerable number. Secondly, for the most part the factors represent options; that is, you can choose to project a feeling of, say, being approachable even if this is not your natural inclination. Most people actively boost the way they are seen in some respects. You may reckon you are well organised, for instance, but still want to give an impression of even greater heights of organisation on occasion, or perhaps aim to have a particular person see you in this light.

These two factors go together. You should have clear objectives as to how you want to come over, and work at doing just that. The number of factors that you may want actively to include indicates some complexity, and you need to see the process as one of orchestrating everything to create what you want. This may well include recognising weaknesses. If you are naturally a disaster at self-organisation, then you may need to actually get organised, and develop this as a revised part of the way you operate, rather than just seek to appear well organised. At the same time it is not suggested that the overall impression should become too contrived, especially not obviously contrived, which would quickly become self-defeating. For the most part, all that is necessary is some slight exaggeration of characteristics to ensure they are visible where this is what you want.

Perhaps the obvious starting-point with regard to personal image is appearance: your dress and the other elements of personal 'show'.

Looking the part

It should be said at once that the objective here is not to stereotype you or to remove anything of real character and replace it by a universally bland image. The days of the organisation where every businessman, for example, was expected to wear the same (plain white shirt, grey suit, black shoes and conservative tie) are largely gone, and dress now involves a much wider range of acceptable options. Women too, appearing on the corporate scene in larger numbers and more senior positions than in the past, have wide choice. It is, however, a matter of 'horses for courses' and you need to consider what is suitable. Indeed you need to consider what 'suitable' means.

Some things are universally only sensible. I will take the example of a man (being one myself): clean shoes, a well-pressed suit and a smart tie may always be acceptable. But there are exceptions. If a jacket and slacks are what is worn in your office, so be it – wearing that in a well-turned-out way may be fine.

On the other hand there is no option but to make individual judgements. If you work in an advertising agency or some other creative company, then a suit, particularly a conventional business suit, might be regarded as wildly overdressed. Conversely there may be a good deal to be gained by being the only one in a more conservative group who dares to wear a corduroy suit or a really jazzy tie, so that may be the right action too – for some. The most important thing is to think about it. If you simply emerge bleary-eyed from bed and reach for whatever looks reasonably clean you may miss some tricks. The current trend for 'dressing down' and informal days is fine, but does make more decisions necessary.

There are things beyond clothes that need similar consideration. What you have around you speaks volumes about you. There are many things you have about you that contribute to your overall image. Certainly your office, or workstation, is one major one. It acts as a kind of billboard to those seeking to form judgements about you. Assuming you have an office, then signposts there include:

▌ its location (eg penthouse or basement);
▌ its size;
▌ its purpose (eg accommodating just you, or with a meeting table and chairs);
▌ its organisation (eg tidy or bomb site);
▌ its busyness (eg whether it appears to be a place for work or relaxation);
▌ its contents (eg computer and other equipment);
▌ its embellishments (eg pictures on the wall).

The situation is similar with regard to yourself and your more personal accoutrements. Here again there is no one right approach or single solution to how to deal with any particular area. A balance has to be struck, and you can usefully think about how your present way of working comes over in this respect. The following list is designed to get you thinking about the implications here and perhaps prompt you to think of those factors that you can yourself adjust or arrange to help create the positive image you want.

▌ The best computer on your desk may be good, but can you work it?
▌ Are six e mail addresses making you look more important or pretentious?
▌ Is a fat Filofax best or a slim one?
▌ Does your electronic organiser really save you time, or will being seen to wipe out all of your telephone number list one day make you look less than efficient?
▌ Should certificates (linked to membership of a professional institute, say) be on show?

The totality of everything about you – including your choice of company car, hotels you stay in when away on business, even which class you travel on planes and trains – all plays a part in creating the image you present to others. While you can certainly become too contrived about this sort of thing, it is likely to be worse to give it too little consideration.

Each factor is worth thinking about. It is surely true, for example, that you are more likely to deliver appropriate results if you are well organised. Furthermore, you are more likely to be taken seriously if you are seen to be well organised. Consider some examples of practice that gives a positive impression:

▌ *Punctuality*. Turning up for things on time and hitting deadlines take some effort, but are worth while in terms of the impression of efficiency they create.

▌ *Time management*. Managing your time, your projects and diary and creating strong productivity are also well worth while. Good time management can increase productivity significantly. So, although there is no magic formula and the secret lies in the details and creating the right disciplines, becoming good in this way is really a necessity.

▌ *Tidiness*. This is about looking well organised. Your office, your desk and your paperwork can all assist you in putting over the image that you have decided upon. Preparation clearly helps.

Rather like a medieval army lining up on the hill overlooking the likely battlefield, you must decide the position from which you operate. Creating a position of being regarded as personally effective, well organised, confident and on top of things makes sense. Whether you want to work quietly and unobtrusively in the background, or lead from the front, how you appear is important, needs consideration and is not a matter to be left to chance.

Appearance – in all its manifestations – should not be dismissed as cosmetic irrelevance. It is an area well worth some thought. There are few rules as to how to proceed, other than that you need to work at it and take and implement a series of considered judgements to get the balance right. If people are going to see you as influential, as a power to be reckoned with in whatever way and to whatever degree you want, then the sum total of the many ways in which others perceive you must be designed to work actively for you. The objective is directly to influence how people relate to you. Simplistically, this means that if you look like a doormat, you tend to get trodden on, and if you appear to have clout, the respect you command increases.

In summary here, always remember:

▌ You only get one chance to make a good first impression (it may be a cliché, but it is true).
▌ The details matter and contribute to the total effect (for good or ill).
▌ Perception is reality; people really will judge you on appearances.
▌ Consistency of overall approach helps to build an image cumulatively, so 'it pays to advertise'.
▌ Appearance and achievement of results go together; it is no good doing well if people never look beyond a false image to see the strengths you have.

Top tasks
Words that work

The advertising agency with which you are a copy-writer has a new client. The first campaign your organisation has created for them is in trouble. The client vetoed the initial ideas and, with deadlines drawing nearer, new ideas are needed fast. In your view the product is singularly dull – a me-too product with nothing special about it. But it must be advertised, and getting this right can secure the account with the agency and have the client recommending you all over town.

Though it is a team effort, the words are primarily your responsibility – something brief, clever, clear, exciting and memorable, which will ring bells with the public and bring awards at the next advertising industry annual 'do'. Think. What should it be?

Networking

There is an old saying that it is not what you know, but who you know that leads to success. There is real truth in this. You need help: allies, mentors, advisers, those whose knowledge, help or support can make your route to the top a smoother path.

Networking is an active process. You need to do the following:

▌ Seek out people who can help and might be useful.
▌ Keep a record of people, inside and outside the organisation, so that you can contact them easily.
▌ Engage in activities that help you mix usefully (just one example is attending meetings of professional bodies).
▌ Regard the process as a two-way street. If you are not prepared to help others, why should they help you? It takes a little time, but it is worth while – to your job and your career.

Competitive and political pressures

Fact You should recognise that, as not everyone rises equally up the ranks of an organisation, there is an adversarial element to your relations with others. Of course people can work well together in teams, but this does not negate the fact that certain people may be in competition, if not for another specific job then to be first to travel along a particular path.

Fact The office without some office politics has not been invented. Office politics has predominantly negative connotations. The phrase itself summons up images of back stabbing, Machiavellian plotting and watching your back. So the only option for those working in an organisation is to recognise this and act accordingly. No one can ignore any of the realities of life and survive for long, much less prosper in what might be called the office jungle.

Managers and executives are judged by results. Success, achieving the required results, may well be a constant challenge. The phrase, 'The only place where success comes before work is in the dictionary', is usually attributed to Vidal Sassoon: whoever said it first, it is usually true. Yet whatever work – hard work – is necessary to succeed, and whatever skills must be cultivated to back up pure application, the challenge remains – and if circumstances and people conspire to make the task more difficult, this cannot be ignored.

Now, let us be clear. There is nothing wrong with healthy competition between people. Many would claim this is good. Certainly it is human nature. Nor is friction necessarily all bad. Indeed it can act constructively. So too with office politics: it can help – or hinder – you. Whatever it does, its effects should never be regarded as 'just happening'. An active approach is necessary to minimise the negative effects that office politics may have on you, and to maximise constructive ways in which it may help you. You need to recognise that:

▌ People have a variety of personal ambitions that could put them at loggerheads with you.
▌ Some people care little how they hurt others in their striving to get on.
▌ Work is not just competitive; it is adversarial.
▌ Appearances can be deceptive (you need to identify allies and enemies).
▌ Forewarned is forearmed (you need to observe, plan, actively respond and take initiatives).
▌ You need a career plan (if you do not know where you are going, any road will do, as they say).
▌ Perception is as important as fact (how you seem is as much the basis of how you progress as what you actually do).
▌ Surmounting circumstances (and possibly opposition) takes skill – and the appropriate skills must be acquired.

So, a response to office politics must be an inherent part of active career planning. To succeed you need:

▌ to know what is going on (information really is power);
▌ the right people on your side (and to recognise and deal with the 'bad guys'),
▌ good communication skills (this is how you relate to others within the workplace);
▌ the 'right' image or profile (and aspects of this may need creating and maintaining);
▌ the patience of a saint (and the ability to see the broad picture);
▌ sufficient assertiveness (to stand up for what you want and influence outcomes);
▌ organisational and management abilities (to achieve your work and career goals in tandem);

▌ fleetness of foot (the workplace is always dynamic – responding to change goes with the territory);

▌ a degree of ruthlessness (but one that does not dent your image).

Some would say women have to work harder than men in this area. Others remember the view of Charlotte Whitton – whatever women do, they must do twice as well as men to be thought half as good. Luckily, this is not difficult. Whatever your sex, office politics is something to be realistic about. It exists. If affects you. And the only practical response is to take an active approach to it. It is not necessary to be aggressive; it is important to be aware.

Your attitude

It should be clear from what has already been said in this chapter that you need to take a positive attitude to a range of things if you are actively to create a smooth path forward. By way of example, consider the following three specific areas:

▌ *Training.* As you cannot do the job or get to the top without certain skills, training is important. Most companies have a reasonable culture of training. Foster it, use it and request (insist, fight for – whatever it takes) the training you need. Being seen to welcome training and having a planned attitude to it will be well regarded in a good organisation so, while you may not always be able to get as much training as quickly as you would like, it should be possible to secure what you need to underpin your career plans.

▌ *Appraisal.* Not every company or every manager undertakes constructive job appraisals (perhaps not least because conducting a good appraisal meeting is not easy). But however they are done in whatever organisation you may work for – make the most of them. This involves:
  – becoming familiar with the system;
  – asking for an agenda and any other details you think relevant in advance;
  – planning for the meeting (a process that goes on in a way all through the period before one);
  – getting and noting written conclusions;
  – making career planning a part of the process.

The main purpose of job appraisal is to make the next period's work activity go well. But it should look ahead also. Appraisal meetings are, or should be, the appraisee's meeting: have your say, make them useful and always approach the whole thing constructively. What comes from them may directly affect your career progress. More detail of appraisal meeting procedure is beyond our scope here. If you will forgive a plug, my book _30 Minutes before your Job Appraisal_ (Kogan Page), which is written for the person being appraised, might be a worthwhile investment.

▌ _Management_. Appraisal is in fact just one aspect of your relationship with management. You will (until you are managing director) normally report to someone. You will also have to work with others, for example others on the same level in other functions. Again your attitude to these relationships should be constructive and two-way. Just seeing what you can get from people is short-sighted. If you want cooperation then it is better to see it as a two-way street. It should also be said here that, if and when you manage others, you need to work at that management. The process takes time, effort and skill. But it is worth while. As a manager you can only succeed through the efforts of your people. Thus they become vital to your success in your job, and therefore to your career. Look after them. A good team is an asset to anyone's career prospects.

Success, and realism

The title of this chapter talks about a route to the top. The term implies that the route takes some time to travel along. Whatever your current position it is as well to set yourself some goals. These can take various forms, relating for instance to:

▌ salary levels;
▌ job grades and positions;
▌ specific types of work or involvement;
▌ ancillary factors (eg travel).

Remember that the possible path ahead may branch; in other words, a number of different routes could take you down paths that give you the experience and rewards you want. It is a good rule not to cut off your options unless you have to. Things – and feelings – change. It may be that something like the arrival of a young family changes your attitude to travel, for instance. But the alternative might be not to ignore routes that put you in a position of being away from home a lot, but to seek relocation and actually live overseas – family and all.

You have to set your sights high, but also be realistic. If you are clear what you want (and remain so despite changing circumstances) then you can chart a course forward. What you do on the way and how you enjoy that is often as important as the final goal. Having a whole list of goals that take you forward is anyway more likely to be satisfying than adopting a more simplistic approach. You may want always to look to an ultimate goal, but it is satisfying to be able to tick off some lesser ones along the way, preferably on a regular basis.

However successful you may be, and however close you get to the top (or in whatever form you reach it), the old adage that success is a journey and not a destination is worth bearing in mind. You want to enjoy the journey irrespective of where it may end, not struggle unhappily for years to achieve a brief period of satisfaction later on. At any particular point you may have a variety of views about what you have done to date and what you want to do next. The 'career overview' in the box, 'Marketing is not for the faint-hearted' (which also acts to give some insight into one specific area of marketing), was given to me while the writing of this book was in progress. It seemed to me to be such a lively example of the ups and downs involved, as well as demonstrating a clear and active approach to career management, that it is well worth while to include it here almost verbatim (and with thanks to Heather Bernini, Business Development Manager for Barnes Menzies French, for allowing me to do so).

Marketing is not for the faint-hearted

I consider myself as one of a rare breed, a survivor. How have I reached that conclusion? Simple really. I have been marketing professional services now for nearly 10 years! Many people outside this unique sector may say 'So what?' but those within it will understand exactly what I mean.

The story so far: my career in marketing accountants began way back in 1990 when the profession was just beginning to feel the waves of change, but was fighting to resist them. Pannell Kerr Forster, then just outside the top 10, chose to open a satellite office in Luton. I was offered the job of Marketing Coordinator. I still struggle with that job title, as coordinator suggests that all activities are predefined and all the person has to do is make sure they happen. Not so! My experience has taught me that the position should be advertised as Marketing Director, as that is what you inevitably become. Pannell's office in Luton did not survive, for many reasons. One – location, although close to the M1/M25 corridor and even in 1990 with promises of train links to Luton Airport. Secondly, there was no way that business in Luton was anything like business in London. Pricing, and interpretation of just where this firm was trying to position itself, could only end in tears. After three changes in managing partners, each brought in from London but none taking the time to really understand what Luton was about, PKF pulled out in 1995 and went back to Central London with its tail between its legs.

However, I learnt a great deal in those five years. I was a non-fee-earner in a firm of professional people, and it was not always a comfortable place to be. I came from a background of marketing Whitbread's most successful brands, Beefeater, TGI Fridays and Country Club Hotels – a fast, buzzing environment full of noisy extrovert people. I went into what I can only describe as a library-style existence. Shut doors, heads down, soft sounds of calculators being tapped. I struggled enormously for the first year, and then began to build networks around me to help me survive. Outside was where I could be myself, meeting people, organising events, in the Sally Gunnell golden era (the athlete was a then employee of PKF). I was able to meet her and use her for promotional events. We lunched bank managers and politicians. Edwina Currie was a guest in our boardroom for lunch, and I had the questionable 'privilege' of holding her jacket while she visited the ladies! I discovered quite early on that the marketing role was very much an internal one as well as an external one. You need to get every team member on board, or that is the ideal.

You need at least one commercially minded partner who enjoys meeting and talking to people and – warning: there aren't many of those in such a firm, who you can get willingly to make presentations about the firm at events and keep everyone awake at seminars! Lesson number one – if they aren't any good at it, don't let them do it! One horrible memory I have was a post-Budget breakfast event held in our office at PKF when I had managed to get nearly 70 people to attend (a feat in itself). All guests were seated with their plates of kedgeree (a brave decision on menu as the entire office reeked of fish for days afterwards!), when up stood the tax manager to deliver his speech on the Budget. After 10 minutes of trying to get his prompt cards in place and mumbling down at his feet for the next 20, I'm sorry to say I began to lose my hard-earned audience.

Life after Pannells – I then went on to work for Foxley Kingham in Luton, a well-established 30-year-old independent practice. Joy! – my first taste of boot camp, and all the partners had been on it and got the T-shirts (and the baseball caps!) and hundreds of pounds' worth of training materials. Ah, but what was missing? Yes, you guessed it – partner time! They had come back from boot camp so enthusiastic and with every intention of 're-engineering' the practice and what happened? Clients got in the way! No one to pick up the marketing wheelbarrow and carry it forward. In I step. What did I find? Resistance! From almost every team member. The 'change' word didn't sit comfortably with people who had in some cases been with FK for years and years. Why did we have to do anything differently? They didn't come into the profession to 'sell, or worse, ask clients for any more business!'

I really could write a book and maybe, one day, I will! But at the moment this is giving me an enormous amount of satisfaction – and boy, do I feel better.

The greatest satisfaction at FK was achieving a dream. Myself, a partner and a manager set up bds – business development solutions, a division of Foxley Kingham dedicated to helping owner-managed businesses realise their potential – and get a life! (OK, off the back of boot camp, but still no mean feat, as nearly every other practice I met that had been on boot camp were only paying lip service to it.) I was the one who surveyed the clients and asked them what they wanted from us, and quite simply that was it – help to run their business, creative ideas and someone to share their problems with. Within bds I would analyse their business development questionnaires, help conduct planning days and finally offer them marketing services for which I became finally accepted into the sacred inner sanctum of 'fee-earner'. I took Michael Gerber to bed with me (only so I could read the E-myth), and the book _Marketing Professional Services_ became my bible.

Last November whilst on a Steve Pipe 'Added Value Masterclass' conference I unwittingly chatted to two partners from Barnes Menzies French, a business advisory group in Milton Keynes, in the bar before dinner. Later in January they were to headhunt me to join their practice. It took many months of soul searching, before I finally arrived here in July this year. They haven't had a business development manager before, so I am going through the entire process again and quite often asking myself 'Why?' but coming up with the same answer. Someone has to do it, so it might as well be me! There are still too few people who do this job for professional services, which makes those of us who do a very wanted commodity. That however is not enough in itself. You have to have staying power, grit and determination, an ability to stand up to partners and make them listen. You are coach to them and the rest of the team at times, and it can be a lonely journey. I plan to get back to creating a business development division here at BMF – that is the future for medium-size firms like this one. I am still learning, and my job enables me to visit and work with all types of business and learn from that experience. For the future I would very much like to share my experiences with other firms and help them choose the right person for this job, and I think I could do that through one of the ever-increasing independent networks. That is where I see my career path.

Despite difficulties along the way (largely because of the nature of the industry in which she has elected to work), the enthusiasm for what she does bubbles out of this account so strongly that I felt it should be included as a snapshot of the real world.

Now, in the last chapter, we look at some of the considerations in your finding what is the right job for you.

10 Where to find top marketing jobs

Finally, in this chapter are a few words about the process of actually finding and applying for jobs. Whether it is a first job, or a first job in marketing, or you are well experienced and seeking a further step up the ladder or a move to the 'top', how you go about it is very important. Let us spell that out specifically: how you go about it can make the difference between being offered a position and falling at the first post.

This is a well-documented area. There are many books of the 'how to get a job' variety, reviewing in detail everything from the nature of CVs to the right necktie to wear at an initial interview. It is not the objective of this book to duplicate that advice, beyond a brief restatement of certain key issues. Prerequisites of successful job seeking are:

▌ *Prepare a first-class CV.* To this I would add that there is no such thing as a standard CV. By that I mean that often (always?) the CV will need amending to produce the emphasis appropriate to an application for a particular job. This may seem a chore, but it is certainly worth while. Your CV may need to vary depending, for instance, on the industry in which the job exists, the size of the organisation, its location and, not least, the precise configuration of the job, and the skills and experience that it is most important for an applicant to possess. It should logically, given the nature of marketing, concentrate on abilities and achievements. A CV should be neatly typed, which is simple enough with word processing.

▌ *Compose a first-class individual covering letter.* While a CV can be a true reflection of someone's abilities, many are the result of advice and some are written by someone other than the applicant (eg an agency). Employers know this, so in a small, but significant, way the content and tone of a letter can add to the information that is weighed in the balance to decide whether an applicant goes forward to interview stage.

▌ *Be realistic.* Employers use a variety of criteria to make the recruitment process manageable. It is said that the ideal recruitment advertisement prompts one reply – from a candidate who is both suitable and appointed. This may never happen, but the reverse, the job of analysing and screening a couple of hundred replies, is a daunting, time-consuming and expensive task. The result is that requests for candidates are designed to focus the process, securing a smaller number of applicants from those who are exclusively 'on spec'. It is not always the case that a non-graduate, say, to take a simple factor, could not do the job and would never be appointed. Rather it is that when an employer says 'graduates only' it reduces the number of applications and keeps the process manageable. So, be realistic. Apply for jobs that are stretching your credentials a little by all means – nothing ventured, nothing gained. But do not hide the fact that you are somewhat off-spec (it will be seen anyway). Explain why despite this you feel you should be considered and ultimately do not be surprised, or resentful for that matter, if your rate of strike is less with this sort of application.

▌ *Research the employer organisation.* If – when! – you move to the next stage, you really must not go into an interview and ask what the company does! Employers like it if an interest has clearly been taken (it is not so complicated: get their annual report, check their Web site, send for a brochure), and the information you discover can help you decide what kind of things to raise at an interview.

▌ *Prepare for the interview.* This means both checking out good interview practice (it may well not be something you have done so often), and preparing for each one. The latter means thinking through what you might be asked, what to ask, making some notes and aiming to create a link between your experience and credentials and the job itself.

▌ *Be yourself.* There is a danger that all this care and preparation may come over as a stilted approach. Employers want to know about you, the real you. Of course you want to paint a full picture and leave out nothing that might weigh in the balance in your favour, but for all the checking of details, the way your competence shows through the way you present yourself counts for a good deal too. Certainly if you appear hesitant, unsure or appear to be hiding things, that will not help.

▪ _Be honest._ I remember seeing research (by a quality newspaper) that suggested that something like a quarter of applicants lie on job applications forms, and then presumably at interview. Put the best face on things by all means, but resist the temptation to say you were studying for a postgraduate degree of some sort when you spent the time selling shell necklaces on a beach in Goa. It should not be surprising that many employers check; indeed this may be most likely amongst those you would consider the most desirable sort of employer.

Top tasks

Number crunching

Marketing is a creative business, but it is also in many ways as much a quantitative process as a qualitative one. Marketing plans must go hand in hand with financial ones, and with financial justification. Analysis is necessary on a regular basis to enable the examination of the various ratios involved, for example the cost of sales to revenue. It may look at the general situation, product by product, and go right through to the analysis of the profitability of single major customers. Forecasting is necessary too. Prediction is always difficult and will never be 100 per cent accurate, but a best estimate must be made of sales, matched to the needs of production and finance. The business must be conducted in a way that is financially possible. Borrowing money is expensive. Marketing expenditure is in the nature of an investment (simplistically, advertise today and enjoy sales revenue tomorrow) – but realism is necessary too.

You have to fight your corner with the finance director (someone you may feel is uncreative, conservative and all too conscious of the risks marketing apparently wants to take). Are you sufficiently numerate to hold your own and help produce a well-judged way forward?

Marketing applies to you

Remember that presentation is perhaps especially important with marketing jobs. Marketing is concerned, after all, with image, perceptions and how things appear. A potential employer is not just judging you as an interviewee, but inferring from your interview performance how you would come over in other contexts: at a sales conference, at a briefing meeting for major customers or distributors, or when making a case for investment to the parent company in New York.

Beyond this brief comment, we will now turn to the question of where marketing jobs can be found. Locating a job can be low-key and self-contained. For example, I got my first job from the personal initiative of writing direct to a list of publishing companies. Three, out of 30, replied. All said 'No'. But one of those volunteered the suggestion that I try another firm, one I had not approached. I wrote one more letter, and was offered an interview and then a job. Easy – well, reasonably so, as it turned out. But success may not come so easily. As the range of options in terms of the source of marketing jobs is many and various, it may be prudent and useful to use more than one source. This book is not a directory, so no list follows – it would quickly date. Anyway, on the day I wrote this I read in a management journal that there are 4,700 job agencies for executive job seekers on the Internet alone.

What you should be clear about, however, is the range of ways of finding marketing jobs and the differing nature of the different sources. If you are seeking a first job then such methods as university schemes and the job fairs held by universities at which employers set up a stall to attract suitable graduates are good starting-points. Later a variety of other methods is possible.

One point before reviewing methods. It is impossible to know where your next job will come from. To a large extent it is a numbers game. The more bread you put on the waters, as it were, the more likely something suitable is to materialise sooner rather than later. Of course, you may be lucky. Sometimes it happens like that: you see a suitable advertisement, apply and get the job with no more needing to be done. But it is best to assume this will not happen. Consider how fast you need to move. Circumstances differ. You may be content to keep a few things on the boil for some months and see what happens. You may need to spread the net wide to encourage success in the short term.

Avoid one mistake that can cost you a lot of time. That is hanging on for something that looks just right but is slow to come to fruition. It can take time while an application is progressed. You write, you attend an interview, you are put on a short list, you attend another interview, references are checked, you wait... the process can run on for weeks, if not months. It is easy to allow enthusiasm, and perhaps confidence too, to lull you into a false sense of security. You become sure it is 'in the bag'. If the final outcome is not successful and you have not continued other activity so that you have other prospects at, say, interview stage, then you lengthen the whole process. The moral is simple: keeping a number of balls in the air at one time is likely to get you the job you want soonest; and if you end up being offered two, then you can take the best.

Top tasks
First in

You have spotted an opportunity – a gap in the market. It may not happen often, but this, you feel confident, is both new and potentially profitable. You need to make recommendations to the board to obtain funding to investigate and set up a new activity in parallel with existing operations. The cost is significant, the timing is, you judge, important and whatever is done must be effective, and yet effort expended on it must not allow any relaxation in the focus on existing operations.

How can you organise the people and resources necessary and present a plan that will convince others of its merit, yet reassure them that it does not decrease the likelihood of current operations continuing to run to plan?

Back to methods and sources of marketing jobs. Let us start with the least formal:

▌ *Networking.* It is said that it is not what you know, but who you know that counts. It can be true of job seeking, and some people get jobs through the intelligence they pick up from others (and occasionally direct from such a contact). Networking implies a systematic approach to creating and maintaining contact with people, in this case people who might be potential sources of jobs or job-related information. Consider who you know (friends, family, work colleagues past and present, customers and suppliers, professional contacts, competitors – and that guy you met at the conference you attended in London). Keep in touch and consider mechanisms for keeping in touch. Some people you might tell outright – 'I'm after a new job.' Some you might write to, telephone or e-mail. Consider also group situations: where might you meet useful people? One example is at national or local meetings of professional or industry bodies (see 'Useful addresses and information' at the end of this book). Whilst looking for a job, you may want to attend such things a little more regularly for a while, get on to a committee or encourage an invitation for you to be a meeting speaker. Make notes, keep records, plan activity and follow up. Remember that networking consists not just of you seeking benefit from others; it is reciprocal. Viewing it construc- tively as such will ultimately let you get more from it.

▌ *Events.* A variety of events caters for the job seeker, especially at start-out level. These range from the events staged by potential employers in universities and colleges to commercial events held like any other exhibition and typically held in exhibition venues.

▌ *On-spec applications.* This is often rejected as having a low strike rate. So be it. But if you have set your sights on something very specific it does make sense and, provided the approach is professional, can bring success. Timing is clearly a factor here. Given the time, effort and cost of recruitment, if your approach arrives when a vacancy does exist it makes sense for the employer to check you out.

▌ *Media advertising.* The sensible job seeker in any field scours the media. Marketing is a major function of business and is thus a category of job that features in many media. It is worth reviewing the media systematically:

   – National press. The main newspapers to watch are the *Daily Telegraph*, *The Times*, the *Guardian* and the quality Sundays.

- Regional and local papers. These are less used by any but smaller companies. That said, in main centres they may well be worth a look in case something local and conveniently located is missed.
- Magazines. Two categories are worth noting: first, the marketing press (see 'Useful addresses and information'), and secondly, the trade press of particular industries. It is worth noting that the more specialised an industry is (or where people in it regard it as such) the more likely its specialist press is to be used for appointments advertisements. In publishing, for example, _Publishing News_ or _The Bookseller_ are just as likely to be used as national papers.

▨ _Internet advertising._ Here I make a difference between sites on the Internet that display job advertisements, leaving it to the individual to apply direct to the employer, and those (see below) that have an interactive element or describe themselves as agencies.

▨ _Internet agencies._ These have been mentioned before (my having seen research showing that there were nearly 5,000 Internet recruitment agencies in operation). Like so much else to do with the Internet and e-commerce, they change as you watch and no attempt is made here to list even a selection. For all the activity in this sector, the more worthwhile appointments still seem to be more traditionally advertised. By all means search the Web, but you will need to do so selectively or time will allow nothing else. Sites with a narrow focus are perhaps the best priority.

▨ _Recruitment agencies._ These are many and various, and certainly too numerous to list here (details of the definitive reference, a directory called _Executive Grapevine_, appear in 'Useful addresses and information' at the end of the book). Some points are worth making here, however, and to do so from the horse's mouth, as it were, I asked the head of a recruitment agency to comment. Recruitment agencies come in all shapes and sizes. A large general agency may have specialist sections, and deal with marketing as a discrete sector. Others may specialise: by level of appointment, by industry or sector, geographically – whatever. Either may be right for you. Larger agencies offer a broad spread of positions; specialists may focus on the specific area you want. Some recruiters are better informed than others, of course, but it makes sense to start from the basis that you will be in contact with someone who does understand the industry and other details specific to a particular appointment. In the box is a description by Richard Chaplin, of Strategic Marketing Connections, of things as he sees them from the viewpoint of a specialist agency.

Specialist recruitment agencies

Specialist agencies tend to be more cautious over which candidates to put forward. A long list of unsuitable candidates wastes the client's time and is unlikely to generate repeat business. Better to put forward two or three good candidates, and take the time to brief the client in depth. A large agency, by contrast, may be instructed to see if they have anybody interesting, in the knowledge that most of the CVs presented will be unsuitable.

So when preparing for an interview with a specialist agency, expect to be interviewed by a consultant with considerable knowledge of the sector, and who may even have strong links to your current employer. Such a consultant will probably be far more interested in your personality than in a showcase of brochures. After all, whenever a client asks about candidates, most of the questions focus on things not found in the CV. 'What are they like?' 'Will they fit into our culture?' 'How do they get things done?' 'Are they diplomatic in dealing with partners?' A good consultant will pre-empt such questions by making sure that they are covered in the interview report.

I recall a TV programme a few years ago in which individuals were asked to dress in what they believed would be suitable clothes for a job interview for positions ranging from accountant to zookeeper. The results were hilarious. The secret of success is to be professional, in other words avoid ostentation or personal statements such as long hair or short skirts. The primary role of marketers is to make their organisations famous, not to get their own name into the marketing press.

Make sure that you have provided lots of information about yourself to the agency before your interview. For example, we insist that candidates complete an online marketing skills test. This is not intended to catch people out, but to help them understand their strengths and weaknesses, and to see how they compare with their peer group. Personality tests can also be helpful. Are candidates doers or thinkers? Are they leaders or followers? Are they interested in ideas or people? Is their focus strategic or tactical? Is their style extrovert or introvert? How are their relationships with their boss, clients and subordinates? Focused tests can also give guidance on the areas that need extra effort if candidates are to take their career to the next stage.

The intention of skills and personality tests is to enable the interviewer to address the real issues in determining the suitability of candidates for a position:

- the track that candidates are on and where it might lead to;
- the personal and leadership qualities most relevant to future career growth;
- the skills and personal qualities most important in fulfilling their present role;
- the barriers that will prevent candidates from accomplishing important goals;
- candidates' interests, personal motivations and rewards sought;
- the skills that can be translated to another organisation.

Do not be surprised if the consultant does not major on your marketing skills. The specialist who knows marketing in the sector and what the client is looking for will probably have formed a view on your marketing skills from your responses over the phone when setting up the interview. A good specialist agency should also have sufficient contacts in the sector to have obtained basic information about you prior to your interview, particularly when you have been referred by a mutual contact.

Agencies are always on the look-out for talent. Approach them speculatively as well as in response to a specific advertisement.

If they like your CV or any detail accompanying it, they may well interview you. In theory, once you have registered with an agency, they will keep you informed of new opportunities. The Internet is excellent for such matching. In practice, it is best to remind agencies on a regular basis of your continuing availability. Provided they are interested in you, specialist agencies usually need less chasing than larger organisations. If you hear nothing from an agency, ask them why. It is in their best interests to give you an honest response as your comments to friends about them could lead to referrals.

Large or small, the key to a successful agency is individual consultants' understanding of their clients' requirements, and their eagerness to place people. Invest in the relationship with your consultant, and you will be the first to hear about interesting new jobs.

To put these remarks in context, you should note that Strategic Marketing Connections (SMC) was established by Richard Chaplin in 1992. It was the first recruitment agency specialising in positions within professional services marketing. It combines an electronic job bank for junior marketing positions with an executive search service for senior positions. SMC now receives instructions from hundreds of professional firms. It obtains its candidates through a combination of referrals, networking, advertising, an Internet-based vacancy matching service and free career counselling. There is a danger in viewing agencies as 'all the same'. They are not, and nor are the consultants who staff them. You will fare best with them if you remember this, do your homework and tailor your approaches and contacts with them as much as possible.

Headhunters. These are more properly described as executive search agencies. They operate on the basis of taking a brief from employers and 'searching' in an individual way, normally with no formal advertising of any sort, for suitable candidates. They then interview and take the process through as required, much like other agencies. They operate exclusively at senior (or specialised) levels, and their mode of operation is therefore geared to represent employers rather than job seekers. Nevertheless it is possible to register with some of them, though how much use this proves to be is dependent upon the assignments they are commissioned to undertake. If adopting a 'leaving no stone unturned' approach suits, then headhunters may be a group worth pursuing. As with so much else these days, contact is often possible through Web sites. There are too many search firms to list here. However, you might check Spencer Stuart & Associates, one of the large international firms, on www.spencerstuart.com. Their site has a specific facility for lodging your CV with them, and provides an example of how these things work.

■ _Specialist services._ Ways of providing assistance to both job seekers and employers change progressively (as those originating and marketing such services take action to create advantage in the market-place). Internet agencies are comparatively new; further new methodology will no doubt appear. You need to keep an eye on what is happening here and be ready to use the right services when your situation demands this sort of assistance. On the one hand active job seeking demands that you spread the net wide to increase the chances of success. On the other hand you have to be realistic and keep things manageable; compromise again – but do not get yourself into a position where you despair of ever finding the right thing and are just not taking sufficient action to make success likely.

The key here has a strong parallel with marketing a product or service. You must see what needs to be done as 'self-marketing'. You must decide on a suitable mix of methodology and go about everything that it entails in a professional way. You may also need to be persistent and take the long view; your ultimate aim is worth taking both time and effort to achieve.

Whatever you do to get into marketing, and thereafter to get on in it, it is worth while. There are many different things to be done in organisations of all sorts, and many different kinds of people are needed to do them; indeed, believing that accountancy is exciting does not make you a bad person – sorry, I digress. But many would describe marketing as a particularly interesting, potentially exciting and worthwhile career. What needs to be done in marketing is sometimes dramatic, for example launching something like

Playstation 2 or Microsoft's X-Box is always going to be high profile. But getting just one small detail right in a small business is important too, and doing that is also satisfying. A small example makes the point: I bet whoever dreamt up the sign in a camping shop in Stratford-upon-Avon saying 'Now is the discount of our winter tents' felt pleased!

Marketing's role is to make things happen. And it never stands still – creatively and innovatively helping to make it continue to act effectively in increasingly dynamic market-places may be just the challenge you want. Go for it; and when you do – aim high. I wish you well.

Useful addresses and information

Whatever stage of your career you are at you may need information or advice. The following is designed to highlight key sources of information about marketing.

The following entries fall into three categories:

▌ *professional and advisory bodies*: encompassing those that offer qualifications, training, or some sort of appointments service, and those that are simply sources of information and networking (this latter sometimes on a local basis through their regional branches);
▌ *magazines and journals*: containing news of marketing matters, reports and advice on marketing methods and techniques and, in some cases, job advertisements;
▌ *recruitment agencies* (or rather how to access them).

Professional and advisory bodies

Chartered Institute of Marketing
Moor Hall
Cookham
Maidenhead
Berks SL6 9QH
Tel: (01628) 427190
Web site: www.cim.co.uk

This is listed first as a prime source of reference. As an overall summary it describes itself thus:

> The Chartered Institute of Marketing (CIM) is the professional body for marketing, with over 60,000 members worldwide.
> Founded in 1911, it has been instrumental in elevating marketing to a recognised, respected and chartered profession.

It is the only marketing body able to award Individual Chartered Marketer status to eligible members. Chartered Marketer status is a professional standard that reflects an individual's commitment to developing their professional skills in an increasingly competitive marketplace.

As an examining body for over 60 years, the Institute's Certificates and Postgraduate Diploma (DipM) are internationally recognised qualifications, available through a worldwide network of educational institutions and distance learning providers.

It is worth mentioning the following Institute services:

▌ *Career development services*. These include a range of information in booklet form or downloadable from their Web site, a Career Advice Line, a Career Counselling Service (run in collaboration with Connaught Executive via a network of 25 offices around the country and two routes for those seeking new jobs. The first is JobFocus, accessed through the Institute's Web site and available to all. The second (for members only) is the Job Vacancy Database run with Quantum Consulting Group and accessed via www.cim.co.uk/membership-net.
▌ *The library and information service.*
▌ *The qualifications they themselves offer.*
▌ *The network of branches*. These mean no one is far from a local source of information and networking (there are a number of overseas branches also and the Institute links with the European Marketing Confederation with associate bodies in 24 countries within and outside the European Union; total membership is more than 300,000). Their Web site is www.emc.be.
▌ *CIM Direct*. This is a source of business books for purchase.

In addition the Institute is the parent body for the Institute of Professional Sales, which undertakes a parallel role to its parent, focusing solely on the sales function, and in alliance with CAM Foundation (Communication, Advertising and Marketing), which is the umbrella body for qualifications across the various marketing disciplines (www.camfoundation.com). (*Note*: while this is a source of value to all, you should note that some of the services listed above are available only to members of the Institute.)

Other professional bodies include the following (in some cases the name makes any further comment about their purpose unnecessary):

The Advertising Association
15 Wilton Road
London SW1V 1NJ
Tel: (020) 7828 2771
Web site: www.adassoc.org.uk
This represents major advertisers.

The CAM Foundation (see under CIM above)

The Direct Marketing Association
Haymarket House
1 Oxendon Street
London SW1Y 4EE
Tel: (020) 7321 2525
Web site: www.dma.org.uk

The DMA is the trade association for companies in the direct marketing industry. Its mission is to represent the best interests of its members by raising the stature of the industry, and give consumers trust and confidence in direct marketing. It has over 830 member organisations, including many banks, insurance companies, charities, retail stores, utilities and home shopping companies together with suppliers of specialist direct marketing services. Total value of sales generated by direct marketing activities is around £30 billion annually. Total expenditure on direct marketing is around £8.3 billion annually.

Incorporated Society of British Advertisers
44 Hertford Street
London WC2E 9DP
Tel: (020) 7129 5355
The body to which advertising agencies relate.

The Industrial Marketing Association
18 St Peters Steps
Brixham
Devon TQ5 9TE
A small body with a focus on its own specific brand of marketing.

The Institute of Professional Sales
(part of CIM listed above)

The Institute of Direct Marketing
1 Park Road
Teddington
Middx TW11 0AR

The IDM is Europe's leading professional development body for direct and interactive marketing. Founded in 1987, the IDM provides information services, qualifications, training, events and publications to students of marketing and marketing practitioners to enhance their careers and encourage best practice in the profession. The IDM is a non-profit organisation, an educational trust and registered charity.

The Institute of Practitioners in Advertising
44 Belgrave Square
London SW1X 8QR
Tel: (020) 7235 5151
This is the specialist body for advertising agencies.

The Institute of Public Relations
15 Northburgh Street
London EC1V 0PR
Tel: (020) 7253 5151
Web site: www.ipr.org.uk

The Institute of Sales Promotion
66–68 Pentonville Road
London N1 9HS
Tel: (020) 7837 5340

Market Research Society
15 Northburgh Street
London EC1V 0AH
Tel: (020) 7490 4911
Web site: www.marketresearch.org.uk

The Marketing Society
St George's House
3/5 Pepys Road
London SW20 8NJ
Tel: (020) 8879 3464
Web site: www.marketing-society.org.uk

It describes itself as 'the premier organisation in the U.K. for senior marketing professionals and general managers of marketing oriented companies'. It states its purpose as being to provide access to the best network for leading-edge ideas and practice and to inspire and support Society members by encouraging debate and contact between them. It is a long-established and well-respected body (with something of a bias towards FMCG companies). It has a quarterly journal, _Market Leader_.

The PM Forum
Warnford Court
29 Throgmorton Street
London EC2N 2AT
Tel: (020) 7786 9786
Web site: www.pmint.co.uk

This networking group is linked to the journal _Professional Marketing_ and has a focus on the marketing of professional services (and a sister group concerned with financial services marketing).

The Professional Services Marketing Group
PO Box 353
Uxbridge UB10 0UN
Tel: (01895) 256972
Web site: www.psmg.co.uk

This is similar to The Marketing Society, but is exclusively for those working in the professional services sector (firms of accountants, lawyers, surveyors, architects, consultants etc). Its main activity is through member meetings of various sorts.

Public Relations Consultants Association
Willow House
Willow Place
London SW1P 1JH
Tel: (020) 7223 6026
Web site: www.martex.co.uk/prca

The Institute of Professional Sales
This is an offshoot of the Chartered Institute of Marketing (same
contact details), one that bestows some welcome recognition on
the importance of sales within the marketing function. It has its
own Web site at www.iops.co.uk.

Magazines and journals

There are many magazines covering the marketing area, either
from a general perspective or with a focus on one specific
subsection of marketing.

Campaign
174 Hammersmith Road
London W6 7JP
Tel: (020) 8267 4683
The main magazine of the advertising business.

Winning Business
Quest Media Ltd
9 The Leathermarket
Western Street
London SE1 3ER
Tel: (020) 7378 1188
A monthly journal directed at managers and directors controlling
sales teams.

Marketing Business
Exmouth House
3–11 Pine Street
London EC1R 0JH
Tel: (020) 7923 5400
This is the Chartered Institute of Marketing's magazine.

Marketing
174 Hammersmith Road
London W6 7JP
Tel: (020) 7413 4567
A weekly, primarily news, magazine (a major medium for recruitment advertising).

Marketing Week
St Giles House
49 Poland Street
London W1B 4AX
Tel: (020) 7439 4222
The main competitor of *Marketing* (see above).

Revolution
WDIS Ltd
Units 12 and 13
Cranleigh Gardens Industrial Estate
Southall
Middx UB1 2DB
Tel: (020) 8503 7500
Describes itself as catering for business and marketing in the digital economy.

Strategieseurope
2 rue Maurice Hartmann
BP 62
92133 Issy les Moulineaux
Cedex
France
The main cross-Europe marketing journal.

Recruitment agencies

This is too numerous a category to list. However, there is one key reference that is worth mentioning and which is the definitive guide:

Executive Grapevine
2nd floor
New Barnes Mill
Cottonmill Lane
St Albans
Herts AL1 2HA
Tel: (01727) 844335
Web site: www.executive-grapevine.co.uk

This lists agencies of all sorts, and information can be accessed in various ways: by industry, or work area (eg market research), with the exact nature of the firm being made clear. First published at the end of 2000, it is subtitled 'The business of international marketing'.

There is, of course, a wealth of other, more general sources of information without a specific marketing focus. Appointments advertisements appear in a range of journals (for example, *The Economist* carries senior appointments, some of which will be in marketing). Other magazines, for example *Management Today*, may give space to marketing issues amongst other matters. And there are general management bodies, for example The Institute of Management and The Institute of Directors, that number marketing people amongst their members. Other references may therefore be worth checking as sources of support, information and inspiration.

Glossary

At this stage, if you are currently outside marketing or new to it, you will be aware that it encompasses a wide range of activity. Describing this multifaceted activity and the techniques involved in its execution has created a good deal of jargon. If you seek to pursue the idea of a marketing career, or extend the one you are currently embarked upon, then you may well need – as has been made clear through these pages – to study further in a variety of ways to keep abreast of all that is involved. For those at an early stage the following short glossary (adapted from the one in my book *Everything You Need to Know about Marketing*) will, while not attempting to be comprehensive, clarify some of the main jargon terms.

advertising The umbrella term for all persuasive messages in 'bought space', incorporating media from TV and newspapers to bus tickets and litter bins.

advertising agency The specialist service organisation planning, organising and creating advertising campaigns for clients.

advertising budget What some like to see as a bottomless pit allocated to pay for advertising.

benchmarking Comparison with competitors in such areas as quality and service.

brand The product or service and all that goes with it, including its image, summed up in the brand name.

brand extension Using the same brand name across a widening range of, perhaps rather different, products.

brand positioning Accurately relating one brand to its competitors in terms of price, quality and appeal.

brand strategy The method chosen to achieve successfully the objectives set for marketing the brand.

channels of distribution The 'routes' along which it is decided to send a product to market; such routes are variable though many companies regard them as fixed – for example, who would have guessed a few years ago we would buy pizza and bulk quantities of potatoes from petrol filling stations?

commission Payments (financial or otherwise) designed to maximise the effectiveness of the job done by salespeople, agents and others.

competition The enemy, as it were, which you should take a broad view when defining, and which you should never take your eye off for one second.

customer Otherwise the client, prospect or punter, the focus of all marketing attention – no customers, no marketing job.

customer care The umbrella term for everything to do with customer service; can – well handled – be a major factor in differentiating you from competition, but is inherently fragile, and failure to meet customer expectations can quickly lose you sales.

database marketing Marketing using sophisticated analysis of computerised customer and prospect lists to direct marketing action accurately (so when I am mailed as Ms Forsithe, there is really no excuse).

direct mail Promotion by post – a first-class way of selling, despite its 'junk mail' image.

direct response Advertising (or direct mail) that depends on individual direct response – clipping, completing and returning a coupon, for example.

e-commerce The umbrella term for the whole process of doing business on the Internet.

FMCG Fast moving consumer goods, typically what you would buy in a supermarket.

integrated marketing (or communication) The concept of ensuring that marketing is integrated into the other functions and activities of the organisation: an entirely sensible approach and, perhaps sadly, likely to be more effective than locating marketing in an ivory tower and doing everything in isolation.

loyalty schemes Often involve issuing loyalty cards, which encourage repeat purchase and customer loyalty. They range from frequent flyer schemes with airlines to cards that link the customer to a retail group or supermarket chain. They are used not least for the information that their use produces. This creates a powerful database, which in turn allows more precise promotional activity to be deployed.

market map A device for tracking the variety of routes to market and the different kinds of customer potentially involved.

market research The process of attempting to find out what increasingly fickle customers want.

market segment A homogeneous group of customers who have similar characteristics or who respond in similar ways. A segment must be numerous enough to be worth targeting, and accessible – communication and supply of product must be capable of being directed at them.

market share The percentage of the total market for something sold by a particular company or brand.

marketing concept The core maxim of marketing: business can only be successful through appropriate customer focus.

marketing culture The orchestration of everyone in the company in a way that ensures that their different roles truly support the customer focus; and persuading them that doing so is necessary.

marketing objectives The results (financial, share of market etc) that it is decided to target.

marketing planning The analysis and decision that set out what marketing activity will be implemented, how, when, where and by whom.

marketing research This is research that is designed to investigate marketing methods, with an eye on improving how they work. It includes attempts to ascertain the effectiveness of advertising, but can be applied to any detail of marketing activity.

marketing strategy The method selected to achieve the results targeted; the 'route' taken.

marketing tactics The nitty-gritty of day-to-day action that fine-tunes the strategy and responds to market circumstances.

media planning The complex and perhaps uncertain process of choosing where advertising is placed amongst the plethora of media options available in order to get the best results.

mission statement An Americanism that may, nevertheless, be helpful in clarifying corporate intention: it is a succinct statement of organisation values and intentions designed to focus thinking and aid communication and common purposes.

negotiation Starts where selling leaves off, and may make the difference between profitability and being taken to the cleaners.

new product launch A risky business not to be undertaken lightly.

niche marketing Activity focused on very precise segments – the very opposite of all things to all people. Niches are smaller than segments.

pricing theory A somewhat uncertain body of knowledge, not to be relied on in isolation, and linked to the concept of supply and demand.

product life cycle The stages over time that a product goes through, from product launch through growth and on to demise or deletion. Marketing activity must vary in the light of the stage of the life cycle that a product is at, and depending on how it is intended to influence its progress. Long life cycles are preferable to short, if only so that the marketer responsible is long gone by the time product senility sets in.

profit What, in most organisations, marketing is about generating; ultimately, unless the shareholders or owners are financially happy there may be troubles ahead.

promotional mix The range of promotional options that exist; they must be made to work together, not used in isolation.

public relations All those areas of publicity that help create the right image of, and opinion about, an organisation; often abbreviated to PR, which is also used to mean press relations, only part of overall public relations.

relationship marketing Consists of planned, systematic communication to keep in touch and develop ongoing and increasing business from existing customers; a sort of long-term corporate chat-up.

sales forecasting The process of anticipating how the market will buy and what quantities need to be made available to satisfy demand.

sales promotion The plethora of publicity devices that are part of the overall marketing effort, from price reduction to competition, sponsorship and events.

segmentation Recognising that markets consist of subsections with specific and different needs, identifying and focusing as appropriate to win business.

selling Personal, one-to-one, persuasive communication whether done by salespeople or others and whether done face to face or, say, on the telephone.

social marketing Marketing activity carried out by non-profit-making organisations, or rather those that intentionally aim not to make profit. Most often it is applied to those organisations that do something worth while, such as charities, fund-raising and campaigning bodies – even government (in regard to campaigns to reduce drink driving, for instance). There are those who would regard some publishers and authors as being in this category!

SWOT Initials standing for strengths and weaknesses, opportunities and threats; characterises an approach to the analysis demanded in effective planning.

USP Initials standing for unique selling proposition; essentially, what it is about a product or service that makes people likely to buy it in preference to other competing offerings.

Web site Not quite the gold at the end of the rainbow, but the latest, technologically based marketing method – the advertisement, catalogue or source of information about an organisation or product that someone can dial into via the Internet. Increasingly this provides a facility for direct ordering (using a credit card). Large amounts of business are being conducted this way, from purchase of books and CDs to interactive auctions of property. (You can click on amazon.co.uk to order more copies of this book and hardly lift your eyes from the page as you do so. Try it!) A fascinating development, and one where there is every sign of its still being in its infancy.

Index

Page references in *italics* indicate figures